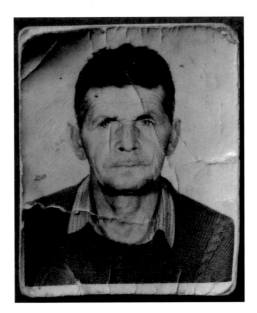

For Erin,

with best wishes.

Patrick McCarthy

AFTER THE FALL

srebrenica survivors in st. louis

text and interviews by **Patrick McCarthy**
photographs by **Tom Maday**
foreword by **David Rohde**
translation and interpretation by **Lejla Susic**

Missouri Historical Society Press–St. Louis

Published in the United States of America by the
Missouri Historical Society Press
P.O. Box 11940
St. Louis, MO 63112-0040

Distributed by the University of Missouri Press
2910 LeMone Blvd.
Columbia, Missouri 65201 USA

www.system.missouri.edu/upress

The Bosnian version of this book is available at www.afterthefall.org

Photographs and interviews from the book will appear as part of
Preživjet Ćemo; *"We Will Survive,"* an exhibit on Bosnian refugees in St. Louis,
at the Missouri History Museum.

Designed by Sam Landers
Designkitchen Inc. Chicago/Los Angeles
www.designkitchen.com

Printed in Singapore

Production of this volume was made possible by a generous grant from the Monsanto Company.

Library of Congress Cataloging-in-Publication Data

McCarthy, Patrick.
After the fall : Srebrenica survivors in St. Louis / text and interviews by Patrick
McCarthy ; photographs by Tom Maday ; foreword by David Rohde ; translation and
interpretation by Lejla Susic. -- 1st ed.
          p. cm.
Includes bibliographical references.
ISBN 1-883982-36-7 (cloth : alk. paper)
1. Massacres -- Bosnia and Hercegovina -- Srebrenica. 2. Yugoslav War,
1991 -1995 -- Atrocities. 3. Genocide -- Bosnia and Hercegovina. 4. Orić family. 5.
Refugees -- Bosnia and Hercegovina -- Srebrenica. 6. Refugees -- Missouri -- Saint Louis. I.
Maday, Tom. II. Title.

DR1313.7.A85 M43 2000
949.703--dc21
                                                    00-035495

foreword
DAVID ROHDE

foreword **DAVID ROHDE**

The pages that follow act as both a window and a mirror. They offer us an opportunity to hear firsthand about one of the great tragedies of our time. And they offer us insight into our own lives, country, and culture.

Patrick McCarthy, by letting Bosnians speak for themselves, and Tom Maday, by capturing images that speak a thousand times over, have compiled a short but potent work. It transforms the confusing and seemingly inexplicable war in Bosnia into something both vivid and understandable. These pages bring into focus the twenty thousand Bosnian refugees who have arrived in St. Louis since the mid-1990s. They put a human face on a distant war and explain the rich culture, fervent family loyalty, and sad history of one of the city's newest and largest immigrant groups.

There is also nuance in these pages. The crimes described are dark, depressing, random, and senseless, but there is also an abundance of human warmth, generosity, courage, and determination. The stories of survival, whether because of the resilience of the victims or the occasional mercy of potential perpetrators, illustrate the importance—not the pointlessness—of individual action.

In their own words, one Bosnian family tells the tale of the worst single massacre of the war in Bosnia—the fall of the town of Srebrenica. This was not simply another foreign calamity where the United States and its allies looked the other way. It was a singular debacle in which the actions of our government and the United Nations abetted the killing of thousands.

With the support of the United States, United Nations peacekeepers stripped the men of Srebrenica of the weapons they needed to defend themselves and declared the small, surrounded town in Eastern Bosnia the world's first "United Nations safe area." But two years later, the UN made little effort to stop an attack on the town and its thirty thousand inhabitants. As UN peacekeepers and NATO jets stood by, the men of Srebrenica were summarily turned over to their enemy or forced to flee for their lives. In all, over seven thousand five hundred men are believed to have perished in a five day bloodletting of ambushes and mass executions.

Five years later, thousands of American soldiers and $1 billion in western aid are being used each year to keep the peace in Bosnia. Srebrenica, ironically, is the most volatile hot-spot in the American sector. Meanwhile, five hundred survivors of the massacre have resettled in St. Louis. Our presence there, and theirs here, demonstrates that our false promises cannot simply be swept into the past. The consequences are with families like the Orićs, and now, with us.

Now, we see them face to face for the first time, and they see us. Their gaze, and their appraisal of their new home, is as unflinching and honest as the face of Eldin Bešić, the young man whose portrait stares from the cover of this book.

The Orić family's perspective on their new home is filled with insights for Americans. Traditional Bosnian hospitality and strong family ties are strained by the need for two parents to work. Children begin to assimilate a new fast-paced, materialist culture and become estranged from their parents. Survivors of a brutal war find themselves unprepared for the pervasiveness of American street crime, and unwitting Bosnian women and children are victimized by a sexual predator.

Some members of the Orić family are disillusioned by their experience in St. Louis and return home, dispelling stereotypes of refugees who never return to their own land. Others stay and soldier on, joining the long tradition of immigrants who sacrificed their own dreams for the betterment of their children.

The story of the Orićs and Srebrenica, I hope, will provoke thought on what America's role should be in the world today. The lesson of Srebrenica is that limited, half-hearted efforts to intervene in foreign conflicts can actually make a situation worse. America clearly enjoys the power to save thousands of lives, but to do so it must intervene with its full force, and with the determination that it will not cut and run at the first hint of potential casualties.

As long as we fail to acknowledge our mistakes in Srebrenica, and as long as the international community fails to bring to justice those responsible for these crimes against humanity, long-term stability in southeastern Europe is unlikely. Thousands of American troops will likely have to remain as long as people there feel justice has not been done.

Imagine, if you will, that seven thousand five hundred residents of St. Louis were missing and presumed dead, and the perpetrators were allowed to live in impunity. As you read the Orić's story, imagine that it is your family abandoning its home in chaos and fleeing for its life. Imagine that it is your brother who was interred with dozens of others in an unmarked mass grave only miles from the small town where he grew up. Read the words, absorb the images, and see that in truth this distant catastrophe was never that far away.

preface

AFTER THE FALL

This book is one story with two parts.

One part is Srebrenica and what happened there.

One part is the Orić family from Srebrenica and their lives as refugees in St. Louis.

These two parts fit together to tell a single story.

This is the story of one place and one family, but it is also the story of why thousands of Bosnians have come to St. Louis as refugees.

This is a painful story of genocide and the human consequences of our failure to confront the evil of "ethnic cleansing" in Bosnia-Herzegovina.

This is also a story of hope and human possibility, of finding strength in broken lives, in remembering and not forgetting, and in recounting and recording lives easily overlooked or dismissed as unimportant.

Finally, this is one way of calling to account those responsible for crimes against our collective humanity.

This project is dedicated to the memory of Haso Orić.

the fall of srebrenica

PART I

narrowing the divide PATRICK McCARTHY

Like many people, I needed a map to find Bosnia-Herzegovina when the war started there in 1992. What little I knew about Yugoslavia came from my high school history lessons. Over the course of the past several years, I have gone from a general ignorance about Bosnia to a deep involvement with the country and its people which has profoundly affected my life and has altered the way I look at the world. The transformation in my understanding began when I met the first few Bosnians who arrived in St. Louis as refugees in the early 1990s. They were primarily survivors of a notorious concentration camp operated by extreme nationalist Serbs in northwest Bosnia in a former mining pit called Omarska, a modern-day torture chamber and killing center. St. Louis was chosen by the U.S. State Department as a resettlement site for these first refugees because of the low cost of housing and readily available jobs. The reception here was unspectacular. A husband and wife who had been imprisoned at Omarska spent their first evening in St. Louis in a bug-infested apartment sleeping on the floor using their coats as pillows.

In 1993, while there were still just a handful of Bosnian refugees here in St. Louis, I went to a talk on Bosnia on the campus of Saint Louis University. The speaker talked about the situation in Sarajevo from where he had just returned. He described a city under siege, where food, water, electricity, and gas were unavailable and where venturing out for basic necessities meant exposing yourself to the risks of mortar bombs and sniper fire. He also talked about people attempting to hang on to a tradition of multi-ethnic living, the very concept of which had become one of the central war aims of those shelling and sniping Sarajevans from the hills and mountains above the city. By then, I had been turning Bosnia over in my mind and was deeply troubled by what I saw happening there. Still, I was uncertain about what I could do to respond. I approached the speaker after the talk and asked if there was a way I could help. He mentioned an initiative called the Bosnian Student Project being run out of New York which was looking for organizers throughout the country to seek scholarships for Bosnian students to allow them to continue their education and to escape the violence of the war and the "ethnic cleansing" of intellectuals and educated Bosnians.

I organized a scholarship at Saint Louis University for a young woman whose studies at the University of Sarajevo had been cut short by the outbreak of the war. Eventually, the modest efforts of our St. Louis Bosnian Student Project grew to include scholarship help for six other Bosnian students and assistance for those among the growing refugee community who wanted to go back to school to improve their English or to recertify professional degrees from Bosnia. From my involvement with the student project, I was invited in August 1994 to join a delegation of

Patrick McCarthy and Eva Klonowski, a forensic anthropologist who exhumed mass grave sites around Srebrenica, meet in Sarajevo with Ibro Jašarević (far left) and Ševko Muratović (far right) from Srebrenica. November 1998.

Americans and Europeans who were traveling to the cities of Sarajevo and Mostar to deliver humanitarian aid and to be a presence for peace and reconciliation during Pope John Paul II's planned visit to Sarajevo. The pope's visit was canceled due to security concerns, but our group arrived safely in Sarajevo, after a grueling overland trip by bus and passage through an underground tunnel that had been dug underneath the Sarajevo airport. I met Bosnian families who had relatives in St. Louis and brought them money, letters, and photographs. I saw up close the human consequences of genocidal violence in Bosnia.

I came back from Bosnia with a strong conviction that more attention needed to be drawn to the massive violence being directed at the civilian population of Bosnia-Herzegovina and that more needed to be done to support the growing refugee community in St. Louis. I spoke in a number of venues and related the details of my trip. I did television and radio interviews. I wrote and published op-ed articles about the situation in Bosnia. I organized assistance efforts and public-awareness programs on behalf of the Bosnian community.

Meanwhile, I immersed myself in Bosnian culture. I studied Croatian at the local community college and learned to speak the Bosnian dialect of the language once called Serbo-Croatian. I read every book, journal article, and newspaper account I could locate on the current situation and past history of the region. I tried to get a more intimate sense of Bosnian culture as I visited new refugee families in their homes. I experienced the legendary hospitality with all varieties of food, desserts, and Bosnian-style coffee. But mainly, I just spent time with people, listening to their stories, lending a sympathetic ear, and offering what practical assistance I could.

As the Bosnian refugee community in St. Louis continued to grow (it now numbers more than twenty thousand), I came to see Bosnians in St. Louis not as an undifferentiated group of "victims" but as people from a centuries-old culture of great sophistication and variety. I learned a lot from Bosnians here about the value of friendship and hospitality. I developed an appreciation for a slower tempo of life. Gradually, I began to look at the world through the eyes of Bosnian refugees and realized that the contribution that I and other individuals could make to the Bosnian community here would be simple human support and friendship. In the process of providing some help in navigating the bureaucracies of establishing utility and phone service, in gathering and delivering donated furniture, and being someone whom new arrivals could look to for help on a small scale, I met and befriended dozens of new Bosnian families.

I was introduced to a family from Srebrenica in 1996 by Ron Klutho, another American volunteer closely involved with the Bosnian refugee community in St. Louis. I arrived one winter afternoon at the door of Juso and Fatima Jašarević, who had come to St. Louis the previous month with their two children, Mina and Hanifa, and Juso's mother, Zumra. I was welcomed like an old friend, sat and had coffee, and began to get acquainted with the family who became the central subjects and participants in this book. I learned that Juso was one of the lucky few to escape the fall of Srebrenica during which the captured males of the town between the ages of sixteen and sixty-five had been massacred at the hands of the Bosnian Serbs. Juso survived a thirty-seven-day trek through the woods from Srebrenica to Tuzla where he was reunited with Fatima and their children. Fatima had come to Tuzla, with Mina and Hanifa two years before to escape the danger and deprivation of Srebrenica. Juso's father and brother were not so fortunate. They perished along with more than seven thousand five hundred men and boys who were killed following the fall of the town.

Within Fatima's immediate family, her brother Haso is still counted among the "missing," the term given to those presumed dead but not located among the thousands of corpses strewn in the killing fields outside of Srebrenica or dumped into mass graves after being summarily executed. The husband of Fatima's younger sister Hatiđa is likewise among Srebrenica's missing. Before I met the Jašarevićs, I had already heard accounts of unbelievable brutality and loss that are the common denominator among Bosnian refugees in St. Louis. Rather than making me feel numb or overwhelmed, these stories deepened my sense of injustice and shame because of the lack of response and attention being paid to what were clearly systematic abuses against the lives and welfare of ordinary Bosnians. The scale of violence perpetrated against the people of Srebrenica made their situation unique, but what had happened to them, sadly, was commonplace in the wartime experiences of Bosnian refugees resettled in St. Louis. And while the presence of thousands of Bosnian refugees in St. Louis represents a significant part of the collective reality of genocide at the end of the twentieth century, the particular circumstances of their lives here have gone largely unnoticed and unconsidered.

By the time I met the Jašarevićs, I understood that nothing I nor any other service volunteer

THE ORIĆ FAMILY

wife, Naza (Salkić)
Deceased prior to war;
no photo available

Suljo Orić
Killed in Srebrenica, 1992

   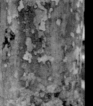            

Hanifa   Haso   Huso   Fatima   Hatiđa   Azra

could do would reverse or lessen the tragedy they had experienced. But I thought that being available to them and helping out in small ways might make a difference in the quality of their lives as refugees in a new and strange place. I got to know the Jašarevićs well and went to the

Hanifa, Huso, Fatima, Hatiđa, and Azra in St. Louis 1999.

airport with them each time a new group of their family arrived in St. Louis. I searched for apartments when the new families arrived, and occasionally, I served as an interpreter for late-night visits to the hospital when a child in the family was sick.

I remember clearly one of my first outings with the Jašarević children. I took Mina and Hanifa and my own two daughters, who are about the same age, to a movie. To kill some time before the movie began, I decided to take the group to a park to play. As I tried to explain our plans to Mina and Hanifa in my limited Bosnian, I clutched the steering wheel with one hand and my Bosnian-English dictionary in the other, trying to drive and look up the word for "park" at the same time. "Idemo u, Idemo u. . . ." Haltingly, I related that "we are going to, we are going to. . . ," grasping at the steering wheel while flipping through the pages of the dictionary only to discover that the word "park" was the same in both languages! We all burst into laughter. We then spent a pleasant hour at the park followed by a movie and a first trip to McDonald's (they didn't like the strange food). Mina and Hanifa's grasp on English quickly outpaced my just-serviceable knowledge of Bosnian. Since then, Mina and Hanifa have become like cousins to our own children. Mina plays soccer and basketball on neighborhood teams with our ten-year-old daughter, and both Mina and Hanifa call my wife faithfully every day or two to ask about a next outing together or when we will come to their house for a visit.

Mina and Hanifa's extended family is the focus of this book. Their mother's family, the Orić family, is from Srebrenica, and like all families from Srebrenica, they have suffered incalculable losses and tragedy. Like most Bosnians, the Orić family has extraordinary reserves of resilience. Their lives are permanently marked by what they have lost, but their lives are not entirely defined by their losses. We present here their story as refugees from the fall of Srebrenica and their lives in St. Louis.

One of the great temptations of our age is to view the world and its people as complicated abstractions, remote from our lived daily experiences. In St. Louis and elsewhere, we are privileged to have an opportunity to encounter those who remind us of who we are and how to narrow the divide between us.

the fall of srebrenica

GENOCIDE IN THE MODERN ERA

Those of us who came of age in the generations after the Second World War and the destruction of European Jewry lived with the belief that "Never Again" meant just that. Never again would the world sit idly by and watch the wholesale destruction of a people without acting to stop it. Certainly, we thought, the enormous evil of genocide could never again appear in Europe, at least not in our lifetime. But it did. It happened in Zvornik. It happened in Foča. In Sarajevo. Banja Luka. Prijedor. Brčko. Mostar. Bihac. Goražde. Žepa. For forty-three months genocide was visited upon these and other towns and cities throughout Bosnia and Herzegovina, towns with funny names, difficult to pronounce, and unfamiliar to the American ear. Nowhere, though, was the pledge of "Never Again" left more cruelly unfulfilled than in a small town in Eastern Bosnia called Srebrenica.

When Srebrenica ("Sreb - ren - neet - sa")—a United Nations–declared safe area—was attacked in July 1995, thousands of Muslim men and boys were slaughtered within hours and days of the fall of the town. Promised the protection of the United Nations, the people of Srebrenica were abandoned by those who were pledged to defend them.

The mass killings that began in Srebrenica on July 11, 1995, ended in the worst atrocities in Europe since the end of the Second World War and recalled the darkest days of the last European Holocaust. Summary executions. Rapes. Torture. Bulldozers plowing killing fields of the living, dead, and dying. When it was all over, more than seven thousand five hundred men and boys were missing and presumed dead. Thirty thousand refugees, separated from sons, fathers, and husbands, were driven from the enclave in an exodus of terror beyond imagination.

What happened in Srebrenica might have been different. In 1993, General Philippe Morillon, the French UN military commander in Bosnia, went to Srebrenica with Serbian military forces on the verge of taking the town by force. Morillon raised the UN flag over the town and declared the city and its refugee inhabitants safe from genocide and under the protection of the United Nations, creating the first of six UN–designated safe areas. The lightly armed Bosnian defenders in Srebrenica were required to give up their weapons in exchange for UN protection. Morillon proclaimed that "an attack on Srebrenica would now be an attack on the whole world." For his courage and heroism, Morillon was recalled from Bosnia, relieved of his command, and reprimanded for overstepping the UN mandate.

Srebrenica was declared a safe area by the United Nations Security Council even though it remained one of the least safe places in the world. Two years later, Serb forces under the command of General Ratko Mladić revealed the false promise of the UN that resulted in the wholesale murder of thousands of people in a matter of days. The architects of Srebrenica's demise, including General Mladić and Bosnian Serb leader Radovan Karadžić, were indicted in November 1995 by the UN War Crimes Tribunal in the Hague for genocide and crimes against humanity. To date, neither has been apprehended. According to statistics compiled by the International Committee of the Red Cross, eighteen thousand persons are missing from the war in Bosnia-Herzegovina. Forty percent are from the fall of Srebrenica.

Srebrenica is no longer referred to as a safe area. With the 1995 Dayton Peace Agreement, which brought the Bosnian conflict to a close, Srebrenica became part of *Republika Srpska*, the so-called Serb Republic of Bosnia-Herzegovina. Apart from supervised day visits under NATO escorts, the ethnic "purification" of Srebrenica is virtually complete. The only Bosnian Muslims in Srebrenica today are the thousands who lie in mass graves in the vicinity of the former UN safe area.

srebrenica
1992-1995 A CHRONOLOGY

srebrenica
1992-1995 A CHRONOLOGY

The chronology of events on the following pages is based on published reports, journalistic accounts, United Nations documents, survivor and witness testimony, transcripts of radio and television broadcasts, satellite photographs released by the U.S. government, and video imagery recorded by Serb TV crews.

JUSO AND FATIMA

Jašarević flee their home in Nurić, near Vlasenica, now under attack by rebel Serbs. They decide to join Fatima's family in the relative safety of Potočari, a town on the outskirts of the city of Srebrenica.

They travel on foot for nearly sixteen hours, carrying their daughters Mina and Hanifa in their arms. Upon arrival in Potočari, they move in with Fatima's father, Suljo, in the family home now occupied by Hanifa, the eldest daughter. Closeby, her brother Haso lives with his wife, Muška, and their children. In another nearby house, Fatima's other brother Huso lives with his wife, Sadika, and their sons. Their youngest sisters, Hatiđa and Azra, are living with Huso and his family.

It is the first time since childhood that they have lived close together. The reunion is short-lived. A month after Fatima arrives, her father Suljo Orić, out looking for food, is badly wounded when he steps on a land mine. His leg and arm nearly destroyed, Suljo survives only a few hours after being taken to the hospital in Potočari. With the death of Suljo, the Orićs are left without either parent—their mother Naza having died some years before the war.

Refugees fleeing Eastern Bosnia.

War in Bosnia-Herzegovina starts as Serbian paramilitary groups begin "ethnically cleansing" Eastern Bosnian towns of their Muslim inhabitants.

The first resistance is encountered in Srebrenica, where the local Bosnian militia repels the Serb attack and regains control of the town.

Surrounding areas fall to attacking Serb troops, and the Srebrenica enclave swells from a prewar population of eight thousand to forty thousand with displaced refugees from other towns and cities in Eastern Bosnia.

srebrenica 1992

Refugees crowd Srebrenica.

The refugee population of Srebrenica swells to sixty thousand. Serb attacks on the town continue and intensify. UN food convoys to the town are blocked. The local population now faces starvation.

Conditions deteriorate in Srebrenica.

The nearby areas of Cerska and Konjević Polje fall to attacking Serbs.

MARCH 5
Relief supplies are airlifted by U.S. military C-130 cargo planes and dropped by parachute to target zones near Konjević Polje.

MARCH 7
After visiting the area, a physician from the World Health Organization calls conditions in Srebrenica "indescribably appalling" and estimates that scores of civilians are being killed by ongoing Serb shelling.

MARCH 11-13
Fearing the collapse of the enclave and the resulting humanitarian catastrophe, French UN General Philippe Morillon, in charge of all UN military forces in Bosnia, travels to Srebrenica.

UN Commander General Philippe Morillon.

Prevented from leaving by desperate refugees, Morillon declares the town and its inhabitants to be under the protection of the United Nations.

The UN flag is hoisted over Srebrenica, and Morillon declares, "We will not abandon you."

MARCH 18
Bosnian President Alija Izetbegović walks out of UN-sponsored peace talks in New York, saying he will return only when the Serbs halt their attacks on Srebrenica.

MARCH 19
After a nine-day standoff with Serb forces, a thirteen-truck United Nations relief convoy arrives in Srebrenica with General Morillon riding in the lead vehicle. Thousands of cheering townspeople come out to greet the food convoys, the first to arrive in Srebrenica since December 10 of the previous year.

During Morillon's visit to Srebrenica.

MARCH 21

With attention focused on Srebrenica, nationalist Serbs fire twenty-four hundred mortar rounds on the Bosnian capital of Sarajevo, one of the heaviest single days of attack in the war.

MARCH 29

Another convoy of twenty United Nations relief trucks arrives in Srebrenica. A field officer for the UN's High Commissioner for Refugees comments, "The situation remains absolutely critical, and if the world temporarily turns its eyes away from Srebrenica, when its gaze turns back it may be very ashamed to find what remains."

APRIL

Srebrenica is again subjected to heavy shelling. The wounded are tended to without proper medical supplies, and limb amputations are performed without anesthesia.

FATIMA JAŠAREVIĆ

Following the arrival of UN food aid, the empty delivery trucks are designated for use in an evacuation attempt to remove the wounded, women, and children from Srebrenica.

Fatima Jašarević, with her daughters Mina and Hanifa, decides to try to leave Srebrenica on the outgoing convoy of empty UN vehicles. Arriving early in the morning, Fatima and her children manage to find space on one of the departing trucks, quickly packed beyond capacity by people now desperate to leave the Srebrenica enclave.

Fatima's husband, Juso, goes to see them off and follows the slowly moving convoy of trucks as they depart the town. Due to suffocating conditions, three women and two children do not survive the sixteen-hour trip out of Srebrenica. Upon seeing the arriving refugees off loaded from vomit- and excrement-encrusted vehicles in Tuzla, a Bosnian government official complains, "We don't even transport livestock in this manner."

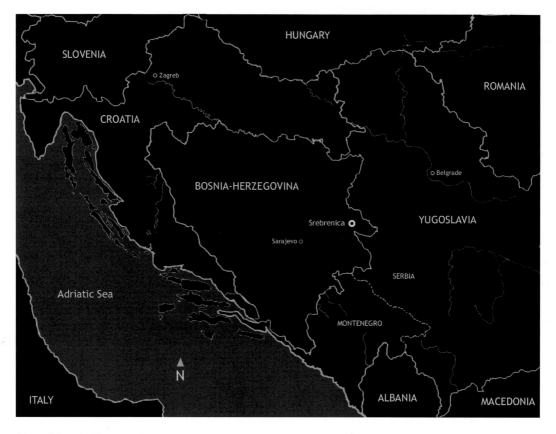

Map of Bosnia-Herzegovina.

By UN Security Council Resolution 819, Srebrenica is designated the first of what will eventually become six UN safe areas in Bosnia. The UN requests thirty thousand peacekeepers to protect the new safe areas. The United States refuses to provide any troops and only seven thousand peace-keepers are sent to the new "safe areas."

1994
Conditions in Srebrenica worsen, as thousands of refugees are forced to live on streets which are running with untreated sewage. Periodic Serb mortar attacks and black market trading in food reduces the Srebrenica enclave to a large "concentration camp."

SPRING 1995
Bosnian Serb forces begin final consolidation of areas under their control in which the Muslim population has been expelled. Srebrenica remains one of three Eastern Bosnian enclaves standing in the way of total control of the region.

UN Observation Post in Srebrenica.

MAY 23-30
Bosnian Serb army seizes heavy weaponry from UN depots. Limited NATO air strikes hit Serb nationalist weapons depot at Pale, near Sarajevo. Serb nationalists take 270 UN hostages and later seize at least 100 more.

JUNE
Serbian army begins to amass troops near Srebrenica. Reconnaissance photos detect these troop movements. The threat against the UN safe area is discounted by the UN command.

JUNE 3
Bosnian Serb army captures Srebrenica outpost.

Bosnian Serb General Ratko Mladić.

French UN General Bernard Janvier, who now directs UN forces in Bosnia, meets Ratko Mladić, in charge of the Bosnian Serb military forces.

Mladić proposes the release of UN hostages in exchange for Janvier's pledge to end NATO air attacks against Serb forces. Janvier says he will take the proposal to his superiors.

JUNE 7
Serb nationalists release 111 hostages.

UN Representative Yasushi Akashi and UN Military Commander Bernard Janvier.

UN Special Representative in Bosnia, Yasushi Akashi, announces UN will abide "strictly by peace-keeping principles," that is, no use of force.

JUNE 13-18
Serb nationalists release all remaining hostages.

JUNE 24
Serb army threatens to "demilitarize" the UN safe area of Srebrenica, but threats are not taken seriously.

Dutch request for air strikes (July 6).

The attack on Srebrenica begins at 3:15 A.M. with heavy shelling of civilian targets by tanks and artillery.

Serb forces, 1.2 miles from the center of Srebrenica, overrun five of the thirteen Dutch observation posts.

Dutch UN battalion commander in Srebrenica asks that NATO planes be readied for air attacks against Serbs invading Srebrenica.

Citing new guidelines issued by General Janvier restricting the use of NATO air attacks, the UN commander in Sarajevo vetoes the request.

UN military observers appeal to the United Nations to "stop this carnage and damage to the civilian property in a UN-declared safe zone."

The observers' commander in nearby Tuzla issues a report asserting it was "very unlikely" that the Serbs "intend to launch a full-scale attack" because "liquidation of a registered population of this size would be impossible," and removal of the population would be impossible without UN cooperation.

JULY 8

UN observers report that shelling has resumed and was at its "utmost height . . . without any sign of abating."

Serbian troops move against UN observation posts in Srebrenica, forcing the withdrawal of Dutch troops.

The Dutch abandon three posts under direct fire, and thirty Dutch troops are taken off by Serbs to nearby Bratunac. The observers urge the United Nations "to find a means of preventing a total massacre." They sign off: "We are now heading for the bunker."

JULY 9

Refugees from the surrounding area begin flooding into Srebrenica.

With more than three dozen Dutch now in Serb hands, the Dutch again ask for air power. The senior UN general in Sarajevo replies that Janvier's command has informed him, "Before we use the ultimate weapon, we should react with a lower level of force."

Dutch UN troops are ordered to take up "blocking positions" to prevent a Serb advance on the town.

JULY 10

Top military and civilian staff at UN headquarters in Zagreb hold a crisis meeting at which now almost everyone, including one of Janvier's aides, calls for urgent air support. But Akashi informs the UN headquarters that Janvier has blocked air power because "the fighting was by infantry, thus making means other than air power preferable."

In response to continuing Serb attacks, the Dutch battalion commander again requests close air support. The requests are again denied.

General Janvier tells his staff that he has spoken to a Serb general who promises him that the Serbs will not take Srebrenica. "I believe him," Janvier says.

The Serb advance continues.

JULY 11

At 1:00 A.M., the Dutch commander is informed by UN officials in Sarajevo that his request for air attacks has been approved. He tells the local Bosnian leadership to clear the area as it will become a "zone of death" from attacking NATO planes.

Serb army in Srebrenica.

The promised air strikes do not take place. The Serb advance on Srebrenica continues.

That afternoon, at 2:40 P.M., air strikes are finally launched but with orders to hit only tanks and artillery pieces seen firing. Two NATO F-16s drop unguided bombs. They miss their targets, two Serb tanks. NATO planes withdraw.

A commentator later writes, "It was like opening an umbrella in a hurricane."

In response, Serbs threaten to kill Dutch peacekeepers; the Dutch government asks NATO to suspend further air strikes.

Now fearing the worst, the able-bodied male population of the town, a column of people that U.S. officials later estimate to be twelve to fourteen thousand men and boys, some of them armed, set off on foot in hopes of reaching government territory in Tuzla.

They are attempting to run the "iron ring" of Serb soldiers with heavy artillery now surrounding the Srebrenica enclave. Fewer than half will make it. Most are ambushed and executed en route.

6:00 P.M., srebrenica falls:

HATIĐA SALIHOVIĆ,

seven months pregnant with her first child, says goodbye to her husband as he joins the column of men attempting to flee the falling town. Hatiđa goes to the Dutch UN base in nearby Potočari.

Muška Orić and her four children hurriedly bid farewell to her husband, Haso. He takes a medallion from around his neck and places it on his five-year-old son, Elvis. "Take care of the children," Haso says as he leaves to join the other men.

Neither will see their husbands again.

Serb forces enter Srebrenica emptied of its population.

As the town falls, two-thirds of the estimated forty thousand inhabitants flee to the Dutch base camp at Potočari.

Backed by tanks, fifteen hundred Serb troops enter Srebrenica to find it mostly deserted.

Refugees in panicked flight to Potočari.

Dutch UN troops evacuate Srebrenica observation posts for their UN base at Potočari. Refugees frantically fleeing Srebrenica cling to the mirrors and hatches of a Dutch armored personnel carrier.

General Mladić giving orders at the UN base in Potočari.

A Dutch report later notes that the Dutch peacekeepers inside the APC can hear soft, repeated "bangs" of those clinging to the outside of the vehicle, as up to twenty persons are "run over" by the treads of the vehicle.

"We don't know how many were killed," a Dutch officer reports. "They were hanging onto the tracks and the wheel arches, like Indians on a train. It could be 10 or 15, maybe more. No one knows."

Dutch peacekeepers and refugees at UN base in Potočari.

General Mladić arrives at the Dutch UN command post at Potočari, on the outskirts of Srebrenica. Before a Serbian television cameraman, he distributes candy to children among the tens of thousands of refugees packed into the UN compound and offers words of reassurance: "Do not be afraid. Do not be frightened. No one will do you any harm."

Mladić also proclaims on camera, "The moment has finally come to take revenge on the Turks," referring to captured Muslims now at his mercy.

Mladić meets with Dutch UN Commander, Colonel Ton Karremans to dictate the terms of the "evacuation" of Muslim refugees from Srebrenica, now encamped at Potočari.

Karremans later writes that it "became clear that Mladić was operating entirely according to a pre-planned scenario."

Dutch troops are ordered by their commanders to "see to it that the forced evacuation take place in as humane a way as possible."

Women and children moving toward buses for evacuation from Potočari.

At Potočari, hundreds of women, elderly men, and children begin to pass through a cordon of Dutch UN peacekeepers to waiting buses. Serb soldiers direct men and boys to step to one side and are led away.

Men of Srebrenica are separated by Serb soldiers.

Dutch troops do not intervene to stop the separation of the men and boys from the women and other children.

Males are directed to one side and led to execution sites.

Dutch plans to escort the buses quickly fall apart, as Serbs confiscate the vehicles of those attempting to provide escort.

Women aboard the buses now see their husbands, fathers, sons, and brothers on the sides of the road gathered in groups of ten and twenty by the hundreds. Some have their hands raised in the Serbian three-fingered salute or clasped behind their backs.

Other men are seen lying in pools of blood with their throats slit.

MUŠKA ORIĆ

waits to board one of the buses leaving Potočari with her infant daughter, Sajma, and son, Elvis. In the confusion, she is separated from her daughters Hasmira, 10, and Naza, 6, who are now aboard the bus with Muška's sister. The doors of the bus close as it prepares to leave. The women aboard the bus realize what is happening and plead with the Serb bus driver to stop and to admit Muška and her other two children. The driver opens the doors to the bus, but because the bus is filled to capacity, the one place left is on the steps at the front of the bus.

Muška quickly boards the bus and squeezes into the open space on the steps.

Seated with Sajma and Elvis around her, the bus departs. As the trip begins under conditions of panic and extreme heat, Muška's children begin vomiting.

The departing buses are periodically stopped and boarded by Serbian soldiers who demand money from the women and threaten to cut off the breasts of those who have no money to give. At some of the stops, younger women are pulled off the buses and are never seen again.

As reports of possible atrocities multiply, officials at UN headquarters in New York ask Special Representative Akashi to keep them better informed. "There have been no reports of physical mistreatment," Akashi reports July 12. "We have been . . . unable to ascertain if individuals are being moved with or against their will."

The Bosnian army, monitoring the ambushes and massacres as they occur, pick up a radio signal from a Serb unit north of Srebrenica. "We have found a place where civilians are concentrated," a Serb officer radios to his commander. The order is given: "Please shell that place."

JULY 13

Bosnian Minister Hasan Muratović informs American Ambassador John Menzies that Serbs have gathered hundreds of Muslim prisoners from Srebrenica in a soccer stadium in nearby Bratunac.

UN headquarters cables Akashi: "It has come to our attention that the Serbs have separated males of military age from amongst the displaced persons and brought them to Bratunac."

"We are beginning to detect a shortfall . . . ," Akashi reports in a cable to UN headquarters in New York, referring to the thousands of Srebrenica men who were now "missing."

Serb soldiers, including "red berets" from the Serbian Interior Ministry, and, among others, the forces of notorious paramilitary units from Serbia proper, begin large-scale killings of men at various points around Srebrenica.

Many Muslim men throughout the Srebrenica area are captured and transported by truck to central assembly points.

Before boarding the trucks, some of those detained have their hands tied behind their backs or are blindfolded. Once the trucks arrive at these locations, Bosnian Serb military personnel order the Muslim detainees off the trucks and summarily execute them.

General Mladić appears at a number of these sites and issues orders to the Bosnian Serb soldiers there.

At night, the executioners use the headlights of bulldozers and earth-moving equipment (used to prepare mass graves and to dump bodies) to illuminate their firing squads.

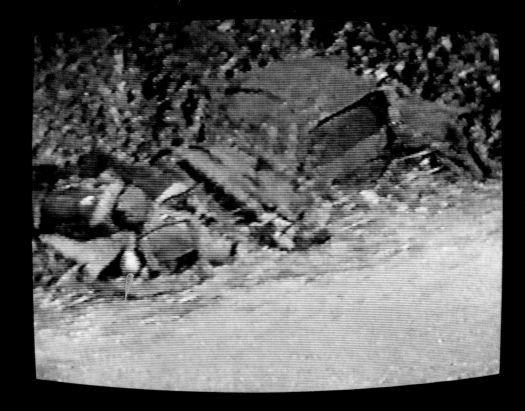

Belongings of refugees dumped on the road side.

JULY 15

In an intercepted phone message, a subordinate to Bosnian Serb General Radislav Krstić reports that he has "three thousand five hundred parcels and no way to distribute them." Krstić says he will help him. The "parcels" are later determined to be a code word for Muslim prisoners.

JULY 16

Another subordinate leaves a message for Krstić that he has "finished the job."

Between one thousand and twelve hundred captured men from Srebrenica are executed on the Branjevo farm in the village of Pilica.

Back in Potočari, Serb soldiers gather the suitcases and other belongings the men have left behind. They are heaped into a large pile and burned.

Serb attack on Žepa begins.

JULY 18

In the area of Nezuk, about twenty groups, each containing five to ten Bosnian Muslim men, surrender to Bosnian Serb forces. After the men surrender, they are ordered to line up and are summarily executed.

UN headquarters, citing "widespread and consistent" reports of atrocities, complain: "We have heard nothing on the subject" from Akashi.

JULY 19

The second UN safe area of Žepa falls.

JULY 20

By now, the majority of more than seven thousand men captured or ambushed in Srebrenica are dead. In a "mopping up" operation near the village of Meces, Serb military personnel, using megaphones, urge Bosnian Muslim men who have fled Srebrenica to surrender and assure them that they will be safe. Approximately 350 men respond to these entreaties and surrender. Bosnian Serb soldiers take approximately 150 of them, instruct them to dig their own graves, and summarily execute them.

Captured boy in Serb custody.

JULY 22

Four hundred and thirty Dutch UN soldiers from Srebrenica arrive in Zagreb and are greeted by cheering soldiers, the Netherlands Defense Minister Joris Voorhoeve, and Crown Prince of the Netherlands Willem Alexander.

Later, during a celebration at a makeshift outdoor bar, drunken Dutch UN soldiers from Srebrenica link arms and begin kicking their legs in chorus-line fashion.

JULY 27

United Nations secretary general's special representative for human rights in the former Yugoslavia, Tadeusz Mazowiecki, resigns in protest over the failure to halt the atrocities in Srebrenica and the international acceptance of the occupation of the former safe area. He accuses the UN of hypocrisy in claiming to defend Bosnia while actually abandoning it.

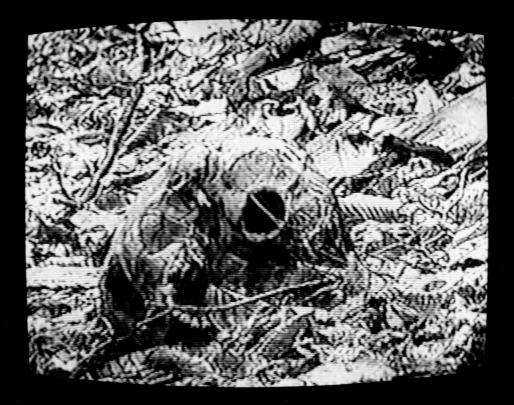

Human skull in a field near Srebrenica.

General Mladić and Bosnian Serb leader Radovan Karadžić are indicted by the International Criminal Tribunal for the former Yugoslavia at the Hague for genocide and crimes against humanity at Srebrenica.

After review of the evidence submitted by the prosecutor, Tribunal Judge Riad confirms the indictment, stating that:

"After Srebrenica fell to besieging Serbian forces in July 1995, a truly terrible massacre of the Muslim population appears to have taken place. The evidence tendered by the prosecutor describes scenes of unimaginable savagery: thousands of men executed and buried in mass graves, hundreds of men buried alive, men and women mutilated and slaughtered, children killed before their mothers' eyes, a grandfather forced to eat the liver of his own grandson.

These are truly scenes from hell, written on the darkest pages of human history."

after the fall:
PART II
THE ORIĆ FAMILY IN ST. LOUIS

BOSNIA-HERZEGOVINA

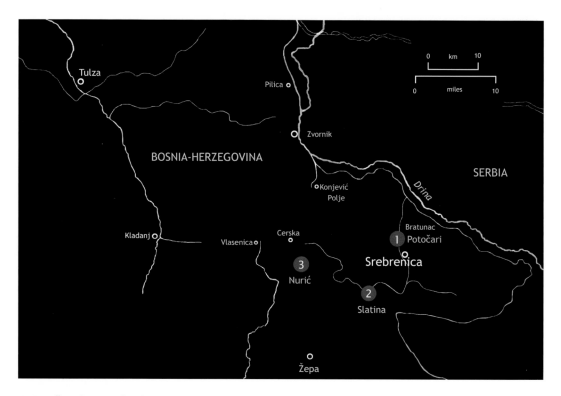

1. Potočari: home of Suljo, Haso, Huso, and Hatiđa
2. Slatina: home of Hanifa and Azra
3. Nurić: home of Fatima

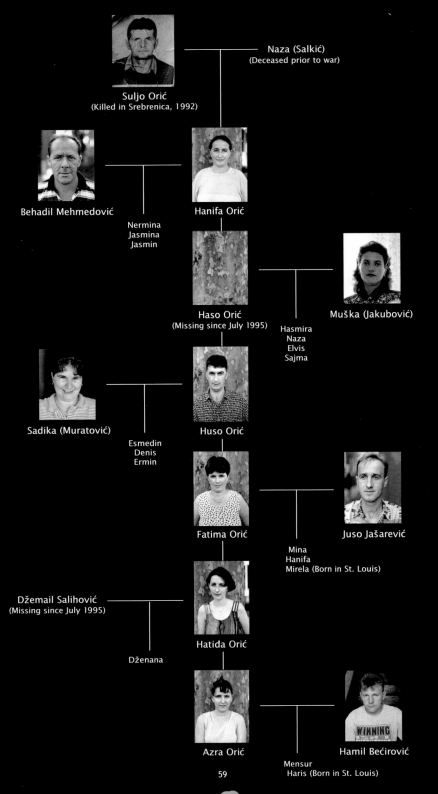

Naza (Salkić)
(Deceased prior to war)

Suljo Orić
(Killed in Srebrenica, 1992)

Behadil Mehmedović

Hanifa Orić

Nermina
Jasmina
Jasmin

Haso Orić
(Missing since July 1995)

Muška (Jakubović)

Hasmira
Naza
Elvis
Sajma

Sadika (Muratović)

Huso Orić

Esmedin
Denis
Ermin

Fatima Orić

Juso Jašarević

Mina
Hanifa
Mirela (Born in St. Louis)

Džemail Salihović
(Missing since July 1995)

Hatiđa Orić

Dženana

Azra Orić

Hamil Bećirović

Mensur
Haris (Born in St. Louis)

orić-mehmedović family:

BEHADIL

HANIFA (orić)

NERMINA

JASMINA

JASMIN

"It would be a shame if people forgot what happened in Srebrenica."

ORIĆ-MEHMEDOVIĆ

Behadil   Hanifa (Orić)   Nermina   Jasmina   Jasmin

Hanifa: My name is Hanifa. My last name is Mehmedović. I am thirty-six years old and I am from Potočari, near Srebrenica.

At the beginning of the war, I escaped my home and was with my father at his house.

My sister Fatima and my sister-in-law Muška were there. We were at home and the bombs were falling all over. My father told us to bring the children in and then he went outside.

We were all inside, really scared, and suddenly the door opened and a neighbor came in and he said that our father was wounded, that he had stepped on a mine.

Hanifa in front at her temporary home, Kerep, Bosnia-Herzegovina. November 1998.

They brought him home first and then brought him to the hospital in Potočari. Haso and Huso were with him at the hospital. He lived just four or five hours.

I last saw my brother Haso seven days before Srebrenica fell. My older daughter was staying at his house and she was attending school close to his house. When everything started, I came to his place where all of her things were—all of her clothing—and I started to collect her things because we were getting ready to leave, to go in case something were to happen.

Nermina, Hanifa, Behadil, and Jasmina in Kerep, Bosnia-Herzegovina before moving to St. Louis. November 1998.

Haso said to me, "Do you really think it is that easy to leave your home?" I will never forget that. When the Serbs came, it was very hard. We couldn't believe we actually left our place and we didn't know where we were going. We went to the UN base in Potočari. People there were lost mostly; they were just asking each other, "What is going to happen?" People were lost, half crazy.

I thought we would be killed. They had a lot of soldiers there when they came. I was with my husband's relatives but none of my family was there. I saw Mladić there. When the soldiers came, he came with them and he introduced himself to us.

He promised that he would take care of us, that nothing would happen to us, and that he would arrange transportation for us to Tuzla. I didn't wait long. I took the first convoy out. I had

bosnia-herzegovina NOVEMBER 1998

(left) Temporary home of Hanifa's family in Kerep, Bosnia-Herzegovina. (above) Mirsad, also a refugee from Srebrenica, asks about other Bosnians now living in St. Louis. November 1998.

Behadil's father with his granddaughter. November 1998.

my children with me and my sisters-in-law.

They would stop the bus and they would shout at us and throw stones. I remember they said, "Go to Tuzla. We'll see you there."

Nobody said a word on the bus. A few cried, the others were quiet. I didn't even think about looking out the window.

We went in the direction of Kladanj. From Kladanj to Tuzla, we traveled on buses provided by the Bosnian authorities. First, we were at Dubrava. It was horrible. Women were crying, children were crying. Some people just went crazy.

They sent us to different refugee sites, and people were talking amongst themselves and that is how we actually found each other. When my husband Behadil heard we were in Živinice, he came there.

Behadil: I am thirty-nine years and I was born in a little place next to Srebrenica.

It was really hard for me to comprehend that the war would come between people who got along for so long and who lived together—Bosnian Serbs, Muslims, and Croats. I was surprised when the war started. I thought the conflict would have a political solution, but that did not happen.

I worked in a factory in Potočari, about five kilometers from Srebrenica. I lived in one small village, and that's where I was when the war started. My village was two to three hours by foot from Srebrenica itself. When war came, it was a really hard life because people were living with the fact that they didn't know what would happen the next day.

As I recall, Bratunac was defeated at the very beginning of the war. A lot of people moved away—they were expelled—and they went abroad or to neighboring places. Usually people who had houses in Srebrenica would take in refugees and that is how they managed to survive.

When the end came, I was in my village. We had to leave. We started at 7:30 P.M. on July 11. We walked together on foot. I went through the woods and my wife and children went to the UN base at Potočari.

The Dutch had observation posts and they were also a target of the Serbs. Everybody was a target of the Serbian soldiers—they would shoot at every moving thing—and the Dutch themselves became a target.

I went through the woods. I was with my brothers, and during the night we were separated and then we never saw each other again.

We went through the woods. I really felt uncomfortable. I had no idea where I was going and was leaving my own place. We were all attacked. It was a really long way from Srebrenica to Tuzla. It took six days for some people.

I couldn't believe the Serbs intended to massacre all those they captured....I don't remember a lot....

I don't even know why Srebrenica was allowed to fall. I am not a politician who can present ideas like that.

I do know that the things that happened to us should not happen to anyone again, ever.

Leaving Bosnia for St. Louis

Behadil: After Srebrenica fell, we were refugees in our own country. There was no work. There was nothing to do. We arrived in St. Louis on June 3, 1999.

My wife's family is here, and even though my family is still back in Bosnia, I came.

Since I got here, it seems that American people are very pleasant. I haven't seen a lot but so far it is good.

I was aware of what was waiting for me here. In order to survive in this country, you have to be able to work and if you cannot work, it is better to stay at home. Only if you work can you live a decent life here. That is just my first impression. That is what I think right now.

Before the war, we had a lovely life. What I will remember are those good days when we lived all together before the war, peacefully, when you could even sleep outside, in the park. Nobody would come and hurt you, and nobody would come and ask you if you were Serb, Croat, or Bosnian Muslim; it didn't matter. I am going to miss the good days before the war.

I believe that we will go back to Bosnia. I hope so. Because my father is there and my brother's children are there. It was not good for my father to come or my sister-in-law to come because she has the young children and who is going to take care of the children?

Jasmin with family, first week in St. Louis. June 1999.

Hanifa: It is too early to say about St. Louis.

For now it is good.

It could be better.

I am with my family and we'll see what happens later.

I just miss the people at home.

It would be a shame if people forgot what happened in Srebrenica.

"I thought we were going to live together and that we would never be apart from each other, but as you see, there is a higher power."

orić-jakubović family:

HASO (orić) missing

MUŠKA

HASMIRA

NAZA

ELVIS

SAJMA

ORIĆ-JAKUBOVIĆ

Sajma   Elvis   Muška (in back)   Hasmira   Naza

Muška: The first day when I heard a gun shot I realized it was actually happening. People had been saying that something was going to happen and I didn't believe it. When I heard a gun shot, that's when I realized that it is happening, that it really is war.

When the grenades started falling, we escaped the village. It was really bad. There were a lot of people from Bratunac, Zvornik, Višegrad who were coming as refugees to Srebrenica. Sometimes even from Sarajevo—wherever the war caught people, they came to us. It was really hard for those people who lived in Srebrenica to keep up with everyday activities, so you can imagine what it was like for people who came from another place.

In March 1993, my father, mother, brother, and my sisters came to me. We all stayed together to the fall of Srebrenica, until 1995.

Just before the fall of Srebrenica, groups of men got together so they could try to escape to Tuzla. My brother, Hamdija, asked my father what he should do and my father told him, "I can't make a decision for you." Hamdija went with the other men who were trying to escape to Tuzla.

My father decided to go with my mother and with the women and children to the UN base at Potočari. My father got on the bus with my mother and was to go with my mother, but they got separated when they took him off the bus because he was a male. I was on one bus and my parents were on another. They took my father off the bus, but I didn't see him. I've never seen him again.

SREBRENICA FALLS

There was a panic among people. They were scared. Nobody believed it was going to be like it was. We thought this was going to stop but it ended up being much worse. People would say things about what was happening, even make up things. No one really knew what was happening. You wouldn't know whom to believe. Some things were not true.

We thought that we would be protected by UNPROFOR [United Nations Protection Forces]. But as you see, it didn't happen. We were not protected.

The first day when the attack started—that was Thursday, sometime in the morning around 2:00 or 3:00 A.M.—I was in the hospital because my brother's wife had just delivered a baby. I was in the hospital helping her, and the wounded started to arrive.

My kids were at home. I left the hospital when the whole thing started and didn't stop. That was Thursday, July 6, the day the shooting started and we left on Tuesday the eleventh.

My husband Haso wasn't home when I left. His brother came and told me to take the kids and to go with UNPROFOR. I wanted to wait for Haso and I didn't want to leave the house without

Muška with her daughter Hasmira in St. Louis. June 1998.

him. But I was scared by the fact that all of the people were leaving—all of the women and children were leaving. We went down to Potočari and I met a lot of people and I asked them about my husband, but they said, "We don't know, we don't know."

When I came to Potočari, I saw Haso there. He came to me—to us—and he asked me if I had found some money that he had left for us at home but I told that I was looking for it and couldn't find it. He took his silver chain from around his neck and put it on our son, Elvis. He told me to take care of the kids. Then he said goodbye. We were all crying.

Potočari

In Potočari, we could hear a lot of shooting around and they kept telling us that we had to keep quiet and that nothing was going to happen to us. But nobody could tell us if we would leave that place and if we would go somewhere else.

A few people had food, but most did not. Kids were crying. They wanted to eat. I was there with my kids and with Huso's wife, Sadika, and her kids. We slept outside on the concrete ground.

In the morning, I asked someone to come with me so I could go up to my house and get some food from the house. There were two women who agreed to join me and we went there together. My house was open. Everything was messed up and broken. I took some food and brought that food back to my kids.

Around 10:00 A.M., one of my neighbors asked me if I would go with her to her home. I said that I would go with her and we came up the hill, but they were broadcasting something and said that all of the people should return to the area near the UN base. They said they would not be responsible for anyone who was outside the area.

Leaving Potočari

When the buses came, my sister helped me. I was carrying the baby, Sajma. My sister had Elvis, and Naza and Hasmira were walking. I told the girls to hold my skirt and my shirt. The Dutch soldiers were actually holding their hands together to form a line [a cordon], so there was just one narrow space to go through. As we were walking, the Serbs could see who was coming and they could control who was able to get on the buses.

I saw a boy who was taken aside. He was about fifteen years old. They told him, "You go there."

Then I realized the same thing was going to happen that had happened earlier in Bratunac— they said they were going to evacuate people but they were actually dividing men and women in order to kill the men. One grandpa was also taken—he was over seventy-five years old. He could hardly walk.

We came to our bus, the fourth bus. We stopped there and we had to go in there. People who didn't have kids or who only had one child, they were able to board easily.

I told my sister, "We can't get on the bus like this. You go in and I'll hand you the kids."

I gave her the bags. I passed Sajma to her through the window and they said, "Stop! That's it. No more people can get on the bus." But I was still outside with the two other kids.

My sister said, "Please, please! These kids need to come in."

The driver said, "Okay, we'll see what we can do."

The bus was overcrowded. I came in and I didn't have a place to sit. I was standing on the steps at the entrance of the bus. I thought I could manage like that—standing on the bus. One of my legs was on one step and the other leg was on another step. I thought I could make it like that, but I just couldn't stand. I had to sit. The driver had to leave the door open so we could get some air.

Every time he would stop, I was in danger of falling out of the bus. The driver apologized to me and said he needed to close the door so he could go faster and so he wouldn't have to think about me falling out.

The kids began vomiting because of the ride and the heat and the panic. The driver was apologizing that the women on the bus and their children were suffering. He was telling his opinions and saying that he was really sorry.

From Potočari to Bratunac, I saw people taking cattle with them. Across the river, there were three

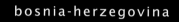

bosnia-herzegovina

houses. A group of Serb soldiers came to the houses and they burned them. The soldiers were throwing stones at the buses, spitting at us, telling us bad things, flashing us the three-fingered Serb salute.

We left Potočari around 1:30 or 2:00 P.M. We came to Vlasenica at night, at 9:00 P.M. We carried the kids and the bags. They told us to stay next to the bus and to go straight in the middle of the road—that we should not go to the left or the right because of land mines.

At one point we sat down to rest. We saw my mother far away with another group. I saw my mother but I couldn't see my father.

My sister told me, "Look, there is our mother, but our father is not there."

My mother came and said that they had taken our father away. After that we haven't learned anything further about him.

Arriving in Tuzla

On July 12, we came to Tuzla from Kladanj. We went to the Dubrava airport. On the thirteenth, my sister came. She had left Bratunac in 1992, just like me. She took me, my kids, one of our other sisters, and the baby of my brother who was only seven days old, and we stayed together in one room for seven days. After my brother arrived, we moved to a school in Kiseljak close to Tuzla. I spent a month and a half there and then went to Gradačac. They were really nice to us there. Everything was really good and I stayed there until the day that I left to go to the U.S.

Searching for the Missing

We were anxious for any information. When each group of men arrived, I asked about my husband, and my sister asked about her husband. We were all waiting to hear the news. One man said he saw Haso before he left Srebrenica but after that nothing more. Whomever we asked, they said, "We saw him the first day when we left." It seemed to me, though, that others were avoiding the subject. They said, "No we haven't seen him, we haven't seen him. Just the first day." They all said they saw him the first day. After that, nobody saw him.

Groups of men arrived in Tuzla on the first day, the second day, the third day, and after a week, up to several months. Whenever a group would come, we would go right there and see who came. I went there every day and I was asking people if they saw Haso.

The day a group would arrive, they would make a list and post it somewhere so we would know from the lists too. A month and a half I stayed to look for him. Whenever someone new arrived, I would go and ask if anyone saw him or if maybe he came and he didn't know where I was. But Haso never came.

To Gradačac

My brother-in-law Huso was there in Tuzla. He arrived after six days and he was in the hospital because he had been wounded in the leg from a grenade. His wife was in Banovići. She didn't know that he was there. He was looking for his wife and kids, but later they met under the tent where Sadika and the kids were.

Gradačac was still taking refugees. Some were concerned because that was still a front-line area in the war. But we decided to go anyway because it was really hard to be in the tents. They would leak when it rained. Huso said I should go back with him to Gradačac and that it would be better for the kids too. So I went there. We had two rooms there.

To St. Louis

My husband's sister was already here in St. Louis. She came after the fall of Srebrenica. I talked to her over the phone and she sent me papers to come over. We kept talking over the phone. I said that I would like to come to America. I said maybe it would be better for me to be in America and that's it. That's how I got here.

Going Back to Bosnia

[In November 1998, Muška Orić returned to Bosnia with her four children and went to Kerep, a

---

(top left) Muška and her brother's family the day Muška left St. Louis to return to Bosnia. (top right) Sajma in a dress at home. (middle left and right) Elvis and Naza playing with a friend outside their home in St. Louis. (bottom left) Muška's coffee table in St. Louis with postcards she was sending home to Bosnia. (bottom middle) Muška with her children. (bottom right) Elvis in his room. November 1998.

Muška's apartment on moving day in St. Louis. November 1998.

small village near Gradačac where they had lived briefly after the fall of Srebrenica.]

The first reason I am going back is that I became disturbed by what happened to Selma. [Selma Dučanović, an eleven-year-old Bosnian girl, was kidnapped and murdered in St. Louis in August 1998 by an American man who committed a series of sexual attacks on newly arrived Bosnian refugee women and girls.]

The man who murdered Selma was at my house before that twice. And I am really upset because of that. It might happen again to my kids. This did not happen in Bosnia.

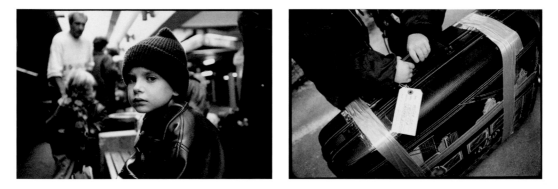

Elvis at the airport the day his family left St. Louis. November 1998.

Second, I am here by myself. It is difficult to support myself and my four kids. We can't pay the bills. I cannot earn enough money for food, the rent, and all the bills. I need to feed my kids, to send them through school, and to get a car. I can't do that by myself. That's why I decided to go back to Bosnia.

REMEMBERING LIFE BEFORE THE WAR

I lived a really good life with my husband. We had a nice good life. Haso worked in a factory. We built our own house. It was all wonderful. Everything was my happiness while we were together before the war. I was so happy when we got married. I thought we were going to live together and that we would never be apart from each other, but as you see, there is a higher power.

(left) In Kerep, Bosnia-Herzegovina, Elvis reunited with his friends. (top right) Muška's mother. (bottom right) reunited family at dinner. (above) Muška with her children, mother, and sisters.

orić-muratović family:

    HUSO (orić)
  SADIKA
      ESMEDIN
    DENIS
          ERMIN

"The most important thing is to find out what actually happened
to those who never came back."

ORIĆ-MURATOVIĆ

Huso (Orić)   Sadika   Esmedin   Denis   Ermin

WAR COMES TO SREBRENICA

Huso: We did not expect it to be like this. We just thought that with these new political parties coming up it would be a little bit of not getting along but not actual war, as it happened.

At the beginning of 1992, the Serbian forces joined the existing Yugoslav army and we were left unarmed. They took over communication sites, roads, and other places from which they could control the city. We realized that was not good.

The neighboring area of Bratunac was already occupied by the Serbian forces. We thought that they would just be expelling the Muslim population from Bratunac. But later we realized they were not simply being expelled but were instead being killed. Rather than resettling the people, the Serbs would kill them on the spot.

A lot of people from Bratunac escaped the horrors that were happening there and they came to our city, to Srebrenica. They told us that a lot of people were killed. They told us about massacres of children and elderly. We realized that something might happen here in Srebrenica and that we should defend ourselves.

We had no way of finding out what was going on outside of Srebrenica because we had no communication connections with the rest of the country.

FROM BAD TO WORSE (1993)

The early part of 1993 was one of the worst times of all. It was not because of fighting but because of the lack of food and other things that were needed for so many refugees. We had an additional seventy to eighty thousand refugees from neighboring places living there in Srebrenica where there was no food and where hygiene conditions were very bad.

It was hard to live day to day since there was no food and the situation was very, very bad. However, the thing that kept people alive was hope—hope that this was going to end tomorrow, or the day after tomorrow. People's hopes went up when the United Nations came to Srebrenica in 1993. That was the time when people thought, "This is going to stop because the United Nations is here."

Morillon entered Srebrenica at this time to defend Srebrenica against the aggressor. It took five days to arrange for his entry. He came in with only twenty or maybe thirty soldiers. Morillon gave a little speech in front of the people gathered there. He said that we should stay calm, that everything was going to be okay, and that we should not make any trouble. I think, in part, he was saying that just so that he and his soldiers could get out of Srebrenica. Our commander asked Morillon not to leave Srebrenica until the UN forces moved in. After Morillon came to Srebrenica, a big humanitarian convoy of food entered Srebrenica and people were really happy that at least they would have a little relief with some food. A lot of women and children got on the convoy trucks and wanted to come out because a lot of people just wanted to get out of Srebrenica. A couple thousand people managed to get out, including my sister Fatima and her kids.

The first UN peacekeepers who came in were from Canada. The relationship between the civilian population of Srebrenica and the Canadian soldiers was pretty good. The soldiers were nice and responsive to the needs of the people there. However, when the Dutch group [Dutch UN peacekeepers replaced the initial Canadian contingent] came in, everything changed.

The Fall of Srebrenica (July 1995)

I was on the east front line, but the Serbs were attacking from the west part of the city. It is interesting that, when the Serbs were attacking from the west side of the city, the UN commander told us to withdraw our forces that were defending the city from the Serbs, since the Serbs were already coming into the city for up to one or two kilometers. The UN commander explained that we needed to do that to make some space for the NATO airplanes that were going to bomb the Serbian forces that were coming in. But that never happened. The air strikes never happened.

The UN soldiers took the side of the Serbs. The goal was to have the UN soldiers keep the city safe from attack by the Serbs, but when the Serbian soldiers began attacking Srebrenica, the UN soldiers were actually siding with them. It may have been to keep them from attacking or to stop shooting, but they were siding with them.

After that, we didn't trust the UN. It was their fault that Srebrenica was in the hands of the Serbs. Since they told us to withdraw our forces, we couldn't go to them and ask for help because we no longer trusted them.

When we realized that the city of Srebrenica was going to fall into the hands of the Serbian forces, we gathered the people who were physically able to walk in order to prepare them to escape from the Serbs. Elderly people, however, turned to the UN peacekeeping forces for protection and maybe a way out of Srebrenica.

We didn't have a choice. There was only one choice. Otherwise, we would have been dead. It was better to go someplace rather than to stay there and be killed.

I was with my brother Haso, my brother-in-law Juso, and my cousins. We left from Sušnjari, toward Tuzla, through Konjević Polje and Kamenica toward Zvornik, and then on to Tuzla. I came to my wife and three kids and we said goodbye to each other. Then she, because she was a woman with kids, she went to the UN and I left with the men.

The Serbs had stationed soldiers at every possible point of exit from the city so we had a very difficult time getting out. We didn't use the road. We went through the woods trying to follow the way of the road but to avoid detection with the camouflage of the trees. This is also how we knew which direction to go.

I was wounded while we were escaping. It was very difficult. I didn't think we would make it out alive. I was able to walk but if we had had a longer way to go and if the conditions for traveling were harder, I don't think I would have been able to come out.

Evacuation from the UN Base at Potočari (July 11, 1995)

Sadika: I was with my children, my mother, and my father. My father was actually still behind in Srebrenica, but a Serb neighbor who was a good Serb found him and sent him to us.

I left right away on the first day when the convoys arrived in Potočari. The only thing I witnessed that made me realize what was going on was a conversation between a Serb soldier and two elderly people—a man and a woman.

The soldier said to the woman, "You leave and let him stay. He'll meet you later."

And the old woman said, "Where is he going to meet me? I want him to go with me now."

"No, no," the soldier replied, "you leave and he'll stay and you'll meet him later next to the river Drina."

I guess, though, that they never met.

There was really no order of who was to go first. Whoever was there closer to the buses would get in. We were in a truck. None of us said anything to the other. We were too scared. Some of the Serbs were cursing us and others were bringing us water and treating us nicely. It was confusing.

People put dimije [a kind of pantaloon skirt worn by rural Bosnian Muslim women] and head-coverings on their young sons to disguise and protect them. Some soldiers said my kids had to get out of the vehicle because they were "men."

Maybe I shouldn't say this, but some of the Serbs were saying, "Look at how many kids you have! It is incredible! Why are you having so many children?"

We went to Kladanj. The Serb soldiers were shouting after us, "Go to Alija! [a reference to Alija Izetbegović, the president of Bosnia-Herzegovina] Go to Naser!" [Naser Orić, the commander of Bosnian forces in Srebrenica] and saying bad words.

Our truck went up to Tišća . From Tišća, we walked. They told us to walk straight, to not veer to the left or to the right because there were mines. We came to Kladanj at night and we slept outside on the grass. The next day we went to Dubrava. From Dubrava, I went to another place and slept in a gym.

ARRIVAL IN TUZLA

When we were in Tuzla, as people began to arrive from Srebrenica, a few people said, "We saw Huso. He's alive."

Then someone else would say, "I haven't seen him." The whole time he was there, wounded and in the hospital. Finally, he found me.

After that, we settled in a village near Kerep, close to Gradačac. We had no work; we were living just day to day. There were a few people who had some work—who had some money—and when I saw them buying things for their children and I was unable to get anything for my children, that is when I decided it was time for us to leave, it was time for us to go to America, to go to a better place.

Huso: It is not bad here. It is a little bit hard if only one parent is working—with three children—but with my wife working too, we can manage. There is work for everybody who wants to work here. But it is hard work.

Sadika: What do I know, but I thought it would be a little bit better for the children here. You really want to work to feed the children, to care for them.

There is no freedom for children here. Freedom means children are safe. In Bosnia, kids would go out of the house, play outside all day, and then come home, and we never worried about them and if they were safe. Because we knew they were safe.

We did not bother with the children to tell them to quiet down, to do this, to not do that, but here we have to do that all the time because the neighbors might complain.

Huso: I miss the Bosnian lifestyle. Before the war, life was easy, pleasant. We lived most of the time. Here we work most of the time.

The biggest differences we see are with the children. We still haven't had a true life here. It is the language barrier. I guess if I spoke the language then I would be able to take the children to some other places, and maybe find a better place to live rather than being here and worrying all the time if I let them go outside.

Already the children are learning the new language and new customs so fast, it will be hard to keep the old customs within them, even those that they never learned. I am glad they have learned the language so quickly so they can teach me, and later on, I will teach them Bosnian, or they will forget the language.

If there was an open life again in Srebrenica, then we would go back tomorrow. If our place, the place where we used to live, would be free of the aggressor, we would return. But I think that if the children wanted to stay, we would let them stay here.

Esmedin at home playing a computer game, St. Louis. June 1999.

Huso: The most important thing is to find out what actually happened to those who never came back, those who never reappeared alive and who were never discovered as dead, those unknown, those people we don't have a trace of. That's the big question. What happened to them? Is anyone going to find out what happened to those people who are not considered dead and who are not alive?

Sadika's father and mother in St. Louis. June 1999.

I really don't know whose game that was—for the city to fall into the hands of the aggressor and for those people to be killed.

Was it the game of the Bosnian government or the game of the United Nations to have this kind of end? I don't know. I'm not sure whose decision that was.

I would just like to tell the world that they have to remember that from ten to twelve thousand people disappeared in two days.

I would like to know how the world could have let this happen. It is something that I just can't comprehend—that so many people would disappear in two days and that there is no trace of them. What did happen, really?

Huso Orić's family in St. Louis. June 1999.

"The baby was born here in St. Louis. Her name, Mirela, is from our word "mir"—for peace and no more war. She was born in peace, in a life that is better than we had in the war.

Mirela means that "the war is over."

orić-jašarević family:

JUSO

FATIMA (orić)

MINA

HANIFA

MIRELA

ORIĆ-JAŠAREVIĆ

Juso   Fatima (Orić)   Mina   Hanifa   Mirela
{born in St. Louis}

LEAVING VLASENICA FOR SREBRENICA

Fatima: We lived in Nurić, in the municipality of Vlasenica.

One day—I don't remember the exact date, but it was in April of '92—Juso and my father-in-law came to the house and they said to get the kids ready and to pack some food and to get ready to go.

It was around 11:30 at night. I had to wake up the children and get them ready to go to the forest. The kids were screaming and they did not want to go, but I had to get them up, to get them together, and to go.

We spent two to three days in the forest. We didn't hear a lot, but on the third day we could hear the grenades and howitzers and bombs falling around, so we had to move deeper into the forest.

We made a temporary shelter with plastic in the woods because we knew that things were happening in Bratunac, Bijeljina, and Zvornik (nearby towns that were among the first to be attacked by nationalist Serbs). The war was already there, so we were expecting the same thing to happen where we were, so we made the shelters.

Juso: We were aware that the war had started in the neighboring places. That's why we got ready. Sarajevo had a few demonstrations, but the real war was happening in Bijeljina.

Fatima: My father-in-law and mother-in-law were with us. It was really horrible. When the bombs were falling, women were screaming, children were screaming—it was really an indescribable situation of chaos.

There were about fifty people together. There was a huge panic. Some people were saying that we should give ourselves up and give up the village. Some people said, "No, we'll never give up the village." There was a lot of disagreement.

My biggest concern was my children, because they were so small. There was one older man who came to us and said, "You don't need to worry about anything because we are going to give up the arms and then we can go back to our homes."

Some people did give up the weapons they had and were permitted to go back to their homes. We were told to put a white mark on our house to tell that we had no arms, that the home was free of weapons. We marked the house in that way when we went home.

We returned home and bathed the children and then did the laundry. We went outside to hang the laundry to dry, and we made coffee and were getting ready to sit down to drink the coffee when the bombs started falling around.

A grenade hit the house. Juso was in one room and the windows were blown out. Juso's father took Mina, our oldest daughter, and he went to the hiding place in the woods.

We all went back to the forest where we stayed for another five days. The kids got sick, and they were coughing and were in really bad shape. My mother-in-law said, "Let's take the kids and go. If we stay here under these conditions, they might die. Let's go back home and if it is destined for us to die, then we'll die."

So we went back home. My brother-in-law came and he told us that the situation in Srebrenica was much better. He said that we should go there, that people were living normal lives there.

Juso said that we should wait until midnight and then pack, get ourselves together, and go.

The trip took sixteen hours. We were really careful. We were also exhausted and when we arrived, we practically collapsed from exhaustion. Juso carried Mina in his arms and I had Hanifa. Juso's arms stayed for some time in the position they had been in while he was carrying Mina.

We went to my dad's place near where my brother Haso and his wife Muška and their kids were also living. Azra and Hatiđa weren't married at that point and they were living at Huso's place nearby.

The situation was much better. There was enough food. The kids got better, and they were able to sleep.

Every day we could still hear the war, but I was inside a house with my family and was as safe as I could be. I thought to myself, "Either this is all going to stop or we are going to get killed." I was fed up with everything. Hunger was coming and I was just tired of it all.

Refugees were coming from other places. They were coming to the outlying areas like Potočari because the city of Srebrenica was already filled up with refugees.

I had been at my dad's place for about a month when he was killed. He went to a neighboring village to get food. He called for me from the outside of the house. He told me to get the kids inside because it was so dangerous. He was walking away and turned around a few times. His last words to me were to get the kids inside so that they would be safe.

Leaving Srebrenica for Tuzla (1993)

It was really hard to divide up the food to feed the kids. If we didn't have bread, we gave them milk. The kids were crying all the time.

We were told that there would be a convoy of food coming and that when they emptied it there would be a possibility to leave and go to Tuzla. I told Juso that I would pack the kids and leave because it was getting harder and harder to feed the kids. Juso agreed and we packed the kids' things and decided to see in the morning if it would be possible to leave.

There were a lot of people there when we came, and it was a big panic. People were getting pushed and stepped on. Some people said that we needed a paper or certificate saying that we were allowed to leave.

Juso came to an empty truck and was helping families load their kids into the truck. We got on that truck. It became so full that Juso was stuck in the back of the truck and couldn't get out. The truck was completely jammed with people and Juso still couldn't move. Eventually, one woman moved enough to allow Juso to get off the truck.

Just after it had left, the truck stopped because there was so much commotion and my older girl, Mina, fainted. Juso was following the truck on foot and when he saw what was happening, he cursed God and said, "You better come out of that truck! If we need to die, we'll die." It was a total panic.

The trip was horrible. At certain points, Serb people threw stones at us and even threw boiling water at us. They said, "What are you doing here? Look at what Naser is doing to you!"

There were three older women and two kids who were crushed to death on the trip. Over one hundred people were packed into each truck. One of the trucks was so full that the back door opened up and people spilled out onto the road.

When we arrived it was dark and we had no idea where we were. Some of the women asked where we were and we were told that we had come to Tuzla. There was a building we went into after we arrived. People there brought us food and asked us what we would like to drink, and the kids were happy about that.

My older daughter—she was seven at the time—asked when they brought the food if it would be all right to keep a big piece of it for tomorrow because she was used to not having food every day. I told her that she would have enough food here and that she didn't need to keep any for the next day.

Juso: For a long time, I didn't have any idea about Fatima and the girls. Eventually, I saw a list of people who had made it safely to Tuzla and their names were on it.

Then I began to get some letters from them, but Fatima was not receiving my replies. She started to ask me why I wasn't writing back, even though I was, but apparently she wasn't getting the letters.

Fatima: One of the messages that I received in Tuzla was from my brother Haso. He joked and said, "You should see us now. We have a new house and some chickens. Convoys are coming regularly with food." I knew that wasn't true at all but I thought if he could joke about it a little, he was probably okay. He liked to joke sometimes. That was my last contact with him.

Juso: I was happy and not happy when Fatima and the kids left. I was happy because that was during the big hunger when there really was nothing to eat. We literally didn't have a single bread crumb.

At the beginning of 1994, things were starting to come down a bit. There was less and less food. Then in '95, it all came to an end.

THE FALL OF SREBRENICA

On July 6, at three o'clock in the morning, they started bombing and we didn't know what it was. We thought maybe they were celebrating something. Usually they would use guns when there was a wedding or some kind of party, but it was getting worse and worse.

The next day we realized that an attack on the town was beginning. It was like playing cat and mouse because at that time our commander, Naser Orić, was not in town. They knew he wasn't there.

The Dutch UN peacekeepers didn't react well. We had to go keep an eye on them. They were pretty scared and we thought they might flee. The Dutch were there to take care of the people, but the people there actually had to take care of the Dutch.

We knew about the possibility of air strikes. But by the time the air strikes came, Srebrenica was already gone.

Only two NATO airplanes came to attack and they only fired warning shots.

When Srebrenica fell, people were aiming toward Potočari on foot. The whole area was abandoned. Even the soldiers, along with the women and children, were moving toward Potočari. If we didn't move at that time, I think we would all be dead.

My father didn't make it. He was with my mother getting ready to leave from Potočari.

Zumra (Juso's mother): My husband, Salih, was at the door of one of the trucks ready to get on. He was getting on one of the trucks and two Serb soldiers told him, "You go there. You are going to take another truck." They took all the men, including the elderly, and sent them to another area. There is a strong possibility that he was killed and that he had his throat slit. That was the area where the biggest number of people were killed in that way.

ESCAPE ON THE TRAIL OF DEATH AND LIFE

Juso: I travelled thirty-seven days before I reached Tuzla.

There was some disagreement between the commanders about who would go, when they would go, where they would go, and those kinds of things. I rested for a short time while this was going on. The first group started leaving at 3:00 A.M. There were so many people that I didn't leave until 11:00 that morning. There were about fifteen thousand of us, mostly men but some kids also.

I was with Fatima's brothers Huso and Haso and my brothers Huso and Hazim. Hazim is missing now, but we were all together at the time. We were ambushed near Kamenica. I lost track of Haso at that point and I never saw him again.

While we were leaving, the first trouble came when a large tree was hit by a shell and fell on a big group of people.

After about two kilometers, there was a second ambush by the Serbs and we were attacked. And about 4:00 A.M. there was a third ambush. There, a friend of ours, Nedžad, was shot through the heart. There was another friend whose head was shattered by a bomb. That was the first time I had ever helped someone who was wounded and I was scared.

There was a plan to go to Žepa, but we were told that Žepa was already under Serb control. Srebrenica fell on the eleventh. On the seventeenth I entered Žepa. For four days, I was in Konjević Polje and it took me two days to get to Žepa. Žepa was still free then, but it fell just a few days later.

When we were in Žepa, we were told to give up to the Serbs. But we didn't do that. We went back into the woods to escape. I was confused, but I knew that I had to take another way out now. My fear was gone. I really didn't care anymore about what was going to happen because of all the things I had gone through.

There were fifty-eight of us together at that point. Mostly people from my village or from nearby, but some also who I didn't know.

On August 2 we encountered another ambush at four in the afternoon. Eight people were killed. Some people got away. We came back to Srebrenica. I stayed until August 10 when they started to "mop up" the area. Near Kamenica, there were bodies all over. Body upon body. It was really hot at that time and the smell was terrible.

Arrival in Tuzla

I asked God to let me get to Tuzla to see Fatima and to see the kids and then die. It had been two and a half years since I had seen them.

Fatima found out that I was there. My brother had told her but she didn't believe him. She was cursing to him, "Don't lie to me!" because a couple of times she had been told that I was there, and it turned out not to be true. She fainted when she went there and found out it wasn't true.

Fatima: I asked a man to take me to where Juso was. I was told that he arrived but that his brother had taken him to another house so that he would bathe and get clean clothes. We went to the place.

There were some men in front of the house. The driver asked, "Hey guys, do you know where Juso Jašarević is?" One said, "He's here."

Juso came out of the room and he said, "Don't cry, I'm alive." He joked and said, "If you are going to cry, don't come to me."

Hanifa, our youngest daughter, was sitting on Juso's lap and kept asking, "Are you my Daddy? Are you my Daddy?" because she had already forgotten him. The girls asked if Juso would have to go back to Srebrenica or if he would stay with us.

Juso: Srebrenica was sold. I am not sorry about the city, really, but about the people. If Srebrenica

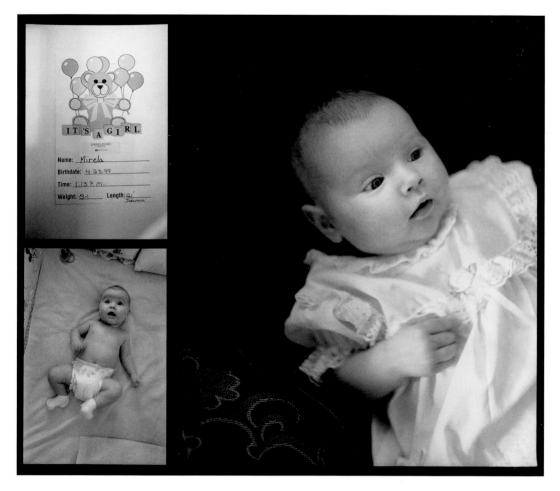

Mirela, born in St. Louis. June 1999.

was to be sold, then they should have taken the people out and given up the city.

Ten thousand people disappeared. The Dutch, NATO, and the UN, this is what they have done. This is their act. They all know.

Juso: I didn't want to come to St. Louis.

There was a big difference between Srebrenica and Tuzla. In Srebrenica we had so little, and in Tuzla there were chocolates and other things beyond the basic necessities. My eyes were popping out at the sight of all that. If you don't see those things for four years, when you see them, it is really incredible.

I thought it would be better in Tuzla, but it was still difficult. We decided to try our chances in America.

I have been here for three years and I still don't feel a need to go back. I miss my family, those who are still alive there and those who died. I have a brother in Sarajevo. I talk to him and he tells me that there is no help for our people, no work, so the situation is really desperate right now.

It is going to be hard for our kids to keep up our traditions. They have already forgotten a lot. They cannot even write in Bosnian. Their English is fine, but when they have to interpret something into Bosnian, they can't.

I want them to succeed in this country. The goal is to make sure the kids have something in their lives.

One day, maybe we'll go back to Bosnia. But after the things that have happened, it is not safe there. We have the kids to think about. Maybe in fifty years, something like this would happen again.

Oh, my Bosnia! Bosnia is no longer Bosnia.

Our plans for now are to raise the kids and to have them get an education.

We have three girls. The baby was born here in St. Louis. Her name, Mirela, is from our word "mir"—for peace and no more war. She was born in peace, in a life that is better than we had in the war. Mirela means that the war is over.

Fatima, Zumra (Juso's mother), and Juso in St. Louis. June 1998.

Juso Jašarević's brother's home outside Sarajevo. November 1998.

(above) Mina hiding. June 1998. (right) Hanifa doing cartwheels in her front yard in St. Louis. June 1999.

oric-salihović family:

HATIĐA (orić)

DŽEMAIL missing

DŽENANA

"Every day, I hope things will get better."

ORIĆ-SALIHOVIĆ

Hatiđa (Orić) and Dženana

THE COMING OF WAR IN 1992

Hatiđa Salihović: There was panic in Srebrenica. Arkan's soldiers [Serb paramilitary forces under the direction of Željko Raznatović, a.k.a., Arkan] had taken control of a hotel in Bratunac and my brother Huso came back and told us we should pack and leave. I was at home with my family. People were saying we should give up our arms and give up ourselves.

I didn't leave my home right away. Arkan's soldiers told us we should give up our arms and our land and if we didn't do that by 10:00 P.M., then they would start shooting. When they told us to surrender, we did not want to. We were told again that if we did not surrender, we would be attacked. Nobody wanted to surrender. The next morning, we were still hoping that they would not attack.

My sister-in-law, my brother, and my father went to my aunt's house. My sister Azra and I stayed at home. That morning I started brushing my teeth, and I heard some noise. Some people started running, and there was shooting all over.

People started running away and when my father saw them, they told him that we should pack and leave too. So we packed and we left. When night fell, we moved away from Srebrenica. My uncle and other people made some shelters in the valley near the river so that we would have a place of escape if fighting started. They made the shelters a couple of nights before when they felt something might happen.

It was raining and snowing. The shelter was leaking and the rain was coming in. It was cold. During the day we came back to the house. The next day the soldiers were coming closer to our house, to our village. My sister Azra and I, my sister-in-law and her children were together. My father and brothers were in the village.

My father was killed [later that year] when he stepped on a mine which destroyed his leg and his arm. We were at home. One man came to us and told us that we should get someone to get my father because the Serbs were getting ready to come in and take him. Our neighbors took some blankets. They went there and they managed to get there before the Serb soldiers came. When they put him in blankets and started leaving, the Serbs came right after them. They were just fifty meters away from the spot where they took him. They brought him home, and when he got there he was asking for water. [He died a few hours later, after being taken to the hospital in Potočari.]

Later I met my husband, Džemail. He was from Bratunac. He would come to our village, to Potočari, and so we met there. There were thousands of other refugees coming from places like Bratunac, Vlasenica, Zvornik, Bijeljina, and small villages and farms near those places. The people who lived on farms and who could grow food had something to eat. But when the food ran out, it was a big problem. Some people died of hunger.

SPRING OF 1993

[In February and March 1993, Cerska (a part of the municipality of nearby Vlasenica) and Konjević

Polje (which is part of Bratunac) fell to the Serbs.]

I remember it was cold, a really, really tough winter. Refugees from these places were living outside on the streets because places like schools where they could be housed were filled up.

There was a game on the playground near where a large group of refugees was housed. They were playing soccer. There was an attack on that place and seventy-two people were killed, and a big number of wounded—I don't remember how many.

I remember the Americans dropping food from planes. The situation got better because people got some food. We thought the situation would improve because we thought the world would do something about what was happening in Srebrenica.

MORILLON COMES TO SREBRENICA

General Morillon came at this time to Srebrenica. He said things would get better. People were much happier when he said that and when he was getting ready to leave, they didn't want him to leave.

There were food convoys that were getting ready to leave after they had unloaded their food, and if you could find a way to get onto the food convoy, you would be happy. My sister Fatima wanted me to go with her, but I couldn't. Fatima left with her children and we thought that they might not survive. We said goodbye at home and then she left. She didn't have much hope that she would get on the convoy, and she thought that she might come back. We told her to take care of herself and the children. She told us the same.

THE FALL OF SREBRENICA (JULY 1995)

People were confused. There were a lot of wounded and dead. I was with my husband. All of us left home together. We came down to the UNPROFOR checkpoint near the gas station. The men went into the woods, and we—the women and children—started towards Potočari. When Džemail was leaving, his last words were, "Take care of yourself."

My brother Haso was living in Potočari. Two days before Srebrenica fell, Haso went to see if the Serbs were coming toward the town. I told him to come for coffee and he said he would stop by on his way back. That was the last time I saw him.

All the people were in Potočari; all of us who were expelled were there. The wounded were inside the fence, those who couldn't walk. [Bosnian Serb General] Mladić was there. He was walking around and would point at the young people who they would take away. He told us if we would like to stay, we could stay and no one would do anything to us.

The Dutch soldiers did nothing. They were not able to do anything. The Serb soldiers took their uniforms and got dressed in them. At one point, we thought those people were Dutch peacekeepers, but then we realized they were not because they were beating us.

Closeby, in Budak, there was a bridge and a river. We went there to get water. We couldn't get water because we saw a lot of bodies of our people there. Those people were not killed with a bullet. They suffered a lot. During the night, you would hear screams, men screaming, and we would hear the noise of machines for cutting wood. When people saw what the Serbs were doing, some people even hanged themselves. It was very, very difficult. People were losing their minds.

Leaving Potočari

There were buses and trucks to transport people from Potočari to Kladanj. I left on the last day. I was with my mother-in-law.

When I was leaving, there was a woman who had a twelve-year-old son and as they got on the bus, the Serbs took the boy.

The woman was screaming, "Let him go! Let him go! I don't have anyone else left." She told them, "If you are going to take him, then take me too." But they said, "We don't need you, we only need him."

A Serbian soldier kicked the woman with his foot and she hit the bus. And her son was taken away.

The bus driver told us that he would not stop the bus anywhere. He would just try to get out of there. He was pretty good because if he would stop on the checkpoints, there might be a problem.

We saw people throwing stones at us as we were passing through Bratunac. I was very afraid of what would happen because I thought I might deliver the baby early.

We arrived in Kladanj. Our driver told us to go straight, not to go to the left or the right, because there were a lot of mines. When we came to our territory, the Bosnians were waiting to take us to another place where we would get food.

Dženana was born twelve days after I arrived in Tuzla. I was in the hospital in Tuzla. I knew that it would be really hard for me to be with the baby and that hard days were coming for me and Dženana.

Life in St. Louis

It was really difficult for me in Tuzla. My sister Fatima told me that when she got herself into a better financial situation, she would send papers for me to come to St. Louis.

Everything here is okay, except for Dženana. She has always been with me; we are constantly together. But here I have to leave her with someone else while I go to work, and I always think about her and what is going on with her. My concern is for her safety and I worry that something might happen to her. When there was peace in Bosnia, we could let our children play outside and not worry about their safety.

If things improve for Dženana here, I might stay. But if I have to fear for her all the time, I think I'll go back. The big difference is that in Bosnia we did not have enough food and clothing. We were always struggling for that. Here it is not a problem—food and clothing. There is plenty of that. But in Bosnia I was free because I was safe. And that is what I miss here—feeling safe.

Before the war, when there was peace, when there was freedom, I would go out with my family, with my parents, with my brothers and my sisters. We would go together to school. Now my father, my brother, and my husband are gone. It is hard without them.

When Srebrenica fell and Dženana was born, she was my only hope. And she is the only thing I have, and if I have to worry all the time about her, I think I might go back.

Every day, I hope things will get better. I just hope that it will be better.

(left) Hatiđa at home in St. Louis. June 1999. (above) Dženana in her front yard, St. Louis. June 1999.

"Everything we built for so many years is gone, is lost. The best feeling is when you are in your own home, wherever that is."

orić-bećirović family:

HAMIL

AZRA (orić)

MENSUR

HARIS

ORIĆ-BEĆIROVIĆ

Hamil   Azra (Orić) and Mensur

Azra: I am Azra Bećirović. I am twenty-three and I am from Srebrenica.

What I remember from the beginning is when my father was killed. There was a field filled with land mines all over and he stepped on a mine that shattered his leg.

[Azra is overcome with emotion and is unable to speak for several minutes.]

Later, in 1993, my sister Fatima left with her kids for Tuzla. We were very sad. Her husband took her to Srebrenica and then he came back and we realized that she had actually left. It was really hard.

I didn't consider leaving. We decided to stay with the rest of the family and we thought and hoped that this was going to end, that this was not going to last. We never thought about things lasting as long as they did. That is what kept us going: that it was going to stop and that it was going to be as it used to be before. And the whole family was there. That was a major reason we stayed.

We never thought the final attack would come. We still stayed in the same place, and we hoped that we would be able to stay there and that eventually it would all stop.

We said goodbye to each other at 8:00 P.M. We were among the last people to leave Srebrenica. Mensur was six months old. We arrived at the United Nations base at Potočari about midnight on [July] 11. There was shooting and grenade attacks all around us.

We stayed there until the next morning, until the soldiers of Ratko Mladić came and they would decide who would go where. We waited for twelve hours and they came around 1:00 P.M., and they were telling us a lot of things and doing a lot of things.

Mladić came in a red Volkswagen Golf. He was distributing juice and food. He told us that women with children up to age one would go first and then we will see what we are going to do with the rest of the people.

His soldiers then came with the trucks and all their ammunition.

General Mladić was giving the children food and said, "Let a *čiko* (a good man) feed you."

His soldiers were also passing out food. They were all very young.

The Dutch soldiers did nothing. We were all together in their area. The Serb soldiers came and took their uniforms and at the end the UN soldiers were left with no guns, so it was pretty obvious who was in charge and who had control of the situation.

We left the same day. The Serbs divided people into groups. They told us that every single group would eventually get out, but we never knew what happened to some of the groups.

I saw them separating men from their families. For instance, a family would come forward to board a bus and if there was a man or an older boy, they would tell them to go across a yellow line and join another group.

We knew the moment that they were separated they would never make it to Tuzla or anywhere else, that they would be killed.

The Dutch did nothing except offer the women the possibility of staying with them, but we weren't sure what would happen if we were to stay.

Our bus went to Tišća, and we walked from there to Kladanj. I didn't see anyone from my immediate family until we arrived in Tuzla.

Our Serb driver said, "People, I don't know anything about what is going on. I am a private transporter and was given an order to come here and to do what I was told."

He was a good man, though. He took a bag of candy and passed it out. He also stopped the bus to get us water.

We thought we would never get to Tuzla. We thought we would all be killed. We thought we wouldn't make it.

We had no idea where we were being sent. Mladić himself had said, "Alija (Izetbegović) doesn't want you." Later he told us, "After we take you out of here, you are going to walk to Alija."

The whole way out of Srebrenica, there were Serb soldiers lining the route. They were just two meters apart. All around—in the woods and on top of trees—there were Serb soldiers. They were saying bad things, but people pretended not to hear.

Hamil: I am Hamil Bećirović. I am twenty-eight years old and I was born in Slatina in the municipality of Srebrenica.

In 1992, March 15, I came back from the former Yugoslav army. I had done my one year of mandatory military service. When I came back to my village, I realized something was going on. There were some soldiers around and something was getting ready to happen.

It was the attack on our village that made us realize that the war had really come. Our village was twenty-four kilometers from Srebrenica. We stayed in our village until Srebrenica fell.

On the twenty-seventh of March 1992, there was a message from Milići, from where the Serbs were living, that we should surrender. We were pretty concerned because previously there had been a little village that had not surrendered and they were all killed or expelled.

Nineteen ninety-two was really a difficult year, and 1993 too, until the food convoys started entering Srebrenica.

Most of the people had worked in factories or had had some kind of industry jobs. Not a lot of people had farms, so they could not feed themselves. When everything stopped, there was no income and no money.

My family was with us, except for my brother who was in Sarajevo. My father died when I was younger but my mother and my brother were there—my brother who was killed in 1992.

He was killed in Srebrenica. It was an accident. He stepped across a trip mine. He was alive for twenty-four hours in the hospital, but he couldn't make it because he lost a lot of blood.

We all lived together in one house. The phones were not working, so getting information over the phone was not possible, but some news was still heard.

March 23, 1993, there was the strongest attack of all, the attack on Cerska and Konjević Polje. The free zone around Srebrenica was getting smaller and smaller.

We heard about Morillon's visit that year. It was really hard because all of those people who managed to escape from Cerska and Konjević Polje went toward Srebrenica. There was an area of about eight square kilometers and there were forty thousand displaced people there.

The situation in our area got worse.

Nineteen ninety-four was a good year in between these two bad years. The situation improved, but in 1995 everything became worse again.

There were humanitarian convoys with food and some farms were getting started, so it was getting a little bit better.

Srebrenica's fall was very sudden. We were in our village when the attack began. There were strong points, strong defenses all around. My brother was with me. My mother, wife, and child were together and they went to Potočari.

Around 7:30 in the evening, we got the news that women and children should go in one direction and that men should go in another direction because of the possibility of attack.

The order came from the brigade commander in Srebrenica and people followed that direction.

It was really hard. My wife took our child and left. I stayed behind at our house and waited for others who were leaving, so that we could go together.

About 11:15 P.M., the men started to get together and we went to a nearby village where the men were also gathering. I was with my family, friends, and neighbors. At one point, there were, I think, something like eighteen thousand men together in that one place.

They told us it would be difficult to walk from the place where we had gathered, to walk to Tuzla, because it was hard to organize eighteen thousand people into one row so that they would go one after another.

People started leaving about 1:00 A.M. It wasn't our time to go until about 6:00 A.M. Those ahead of us were moving for five hours and we still didn't leave until 6:00 A.M.—my brother and the others I was with.

We crossed the Serb line and it immediately became more difficult because we were in their territory. There was one huge group of people walking in front of us, marking the way to go. Of course, after eighteen thousand people go, there is a mark of the way, there was a trail of the way out.

The first attack came in Šitkovići. That was a place we wanted to relax and get some rest because there was still another big part of the walk where there was no place to hide, and so we needed somewhere to wait until night and to rest.

Around 6:15 that night, we started to cross over that field. Around ten people were attacked in the woods. From that attack a large branch fell from a tree. People got scared and they started running away.

I arrived in Tuzla on the seventh day. I didn't sleep at all—a little rest during the day but you could not really sleep. I only had a half kilo of salt and a half kilo of sugar, but some people did have some food. I had a bottle and I would pour water and some salt in it and I would drink that, or I would mix some water and sugar and that was my food.

My only wish was to cross over that area, to get to Tuzla, and to see my wife and child.

We came to Donja Mediđa first and there were some people who were waiting for us and who had prepared food. We were really nicely welcomed. A lot of people there ate too fast, and after having nothing for so long, they ended up in the hospital as a result.

I found my wife and child at the airport in Tuzla. They were sleeping in a tent. We took the bus to a village near Gradačac. We were there for nine months and the people were very good. They offered us food and helped in other ways.

I realized, though, that the situation there was very difficult; there was no work or prospect for the future.

St. Louis

For now, St. Louis is good. It is not what we expected, but it is okay.

There is a lot of work here. However, the quality of life is not as good; it was better in Bosnia.

I wasn't born here and I don't feel like this is my home.

Everything we built for so many years is gone, is lost. The best feeling is when you are in your own home, wherever that is.

There I had my own house. I didn't pay rent to anyone. I only paid for electricity and telephone. What we earned during peacetime was enough to live.

Here it is expensive. Every month we are paying for rent, for gas, water, phone. You must have a car here, and you can't do much without one. These are the major differences.

It doesn't mean a lot that my son was born here. It might be harder for me. It's a plus, but also a minus because I don't intend to stay here and eventually if I want to go back, he may want to stay.

I hope we can go back, but we don't have much hope of returning to our own place, our own home. I don't want my child to have to live through what we lived through.

Everything at home was beautiful—the whole life, especially the natural beauty. Now everything is gone.

Hamil with son Haris in St. Louis. June 1999.

(left) Azra holding Mensur in St. Louis. June 1998. (above) Azra with husband, Hamil Bećirović, and sons, Mensur and Haris, St. Louis. June 1999.

Haris in St. Louis. June 1999.

patrick mccarthy

AFTERWORD

Do you remember on what day Srebrenica was captured?

"July 11."

Where were you?

"At my office in Zagreb."

A black day for you?

"A black day for all of us."

But for you, personally, as head of the UN in Bosnia?

"No, no. It was a sad day, but there were other sad days."

Yasushi Akashi, United Nations Special Envoy for the former Yugoslavia during the fall of Srebrenica, in an exchange with a journalist on the aftermath of the fall of the UN "safe area."

In June 1996, Dražen Erdemović, a member of the Bosnian Serb Army's 10th Sabotage Unit, surrendered to the International Criminal Tribunal for the former Yugoslavia in the Hague. Erdemović confessed to his role in the execution of an estimated ten to twelve hundred captured men following the fall of Srebrenica on the Branjevo farm near the village of Pilica.

Erdemović recounted that, as fifteen to twenty buses with captured men from Srebrenica arrived, his unit was ordered to execute the men. Some prisoners were forced to kneel and pray with their heads bowed, according to Muslim custom, before being shot by firing squads.

Erdemović received a sentence of ten years for his role in the mass killings of men from Srebrenica. On appeal, his sentence was reduced to five years.

Radislav Krstić, commander of the Drina Corps of the Bosnian Serb Army, was arrested in December 1998 for genocide during and after the fall of Srebrenica. Five counts were enumerated in the indictment against Krstić, all relating to the events surrounding the fall of Srebrenica: Complicity to commit genocide; Extermination; Murder; Crimes against humanity; and Persecutions.

In November 1999, the United Nations Secretary General Kofi Annan released a detailed report on the UN's role in the fall of Srebrenica, which acknowledged that "through error, misjudgment and the inability to recognize the scope of evil confronting us we failed to do our part to save the people of Srebrenica from the Serb campaign of mass murder."

In its overall assessment, the report related:

> The tragedy that took place following the fall of Srebrenica is shocking for two reasons. It is shocking, first and foremost, for the magnitude of the crimes committed. Not since the horrors of World War II had Europe witnessed massacres on this scale. The mortal remains of close to 2,500 men and boys have been found on the surface, in mass grave sites and in secondary burial sites. Several thousand more men are still missing, and there is every reason to believe that additional burial sites, many of which have been probed but not exhumed, will reveal the bodies of thousands more men and boys. The great majority of those killed were not killed in combat: the exhumed bodies of the victims show large numbers had their hands bound, or were blindfolded, or were shot in the back or in the back of the head. Numerous eyewitness accounts, now well corroborated by forensic evidence, attest to scenes of mass slaughter of unarmed civilians.
>
> The fall of Srebrenica is also shocking because the enclave's inhabitants believed that the authority of the United Nations Security Council, the presence of UNPROFOR peacekeepers, and the might of NATO airpower, would ensure their safety. Instead, the Serb forces ignored the Security Council, pushed aside the UNPROFOR troops, and assessed correctly that air power would not be used to stop them. They overran the safe area of Srebrenica with ease, and then proceeded to depopulate the territory within forty-eight hours. Their leaders then engaged in high-level negotiations with representatives of the international community while their forces on the ground executed and buried thousands of men and boys within a matter of days.

Yasushi Akashi, when asked if he felt responsible for what happened after Srebrenica fell, replied: *"No. What decision could one have made under these circumstances? Please! We could not have foreseen this, and even if we had foreseen it, we would have been powerless to do anything."*

You feel in no way responsible for the death of eight thousand [Bosnian] Muslims?

Akashi: *"Correct."*

Muška Orić was notified in September 1999 of a possible identification of the remains of her husband, Haso, based on clothing and photographs found with his body. A blood sample has been requested from Huso Orić for the purpose of DNA comparison and final identification.

Seven thousand five hundred and seventy-four individuals from Srebrenica are unaccounted for.

At this writing, Radovan Karadžić and Ratko Mladić remain free.

bosnia-herzegovina
1998

sarajevo

kerep

sarajevo

kerep

kerep

near the border of republika srpska

references
AFTER THE FALL

references and resources for more INFORMATION

BOOKS

CIGAR, NORMAN L. *Genocide in Bosnia: The Policy of "Ethnic Cleansing."* College Station: Texas A&M University Press, 1995.

HONIG, JAN WILLEM, AND NORBERT BOTH. S*rebrenica: Record of a War Crime.* New York: Penguin Books, 1997.

MOUSAVIZADEH, NADER, ed. *The Black Book of Bosnia: The Consequences of Appeasement.* New York: BasicBooks, 1996.

ROHDE, DAVID. *Endgame: The Betrayal and Fall of Srebrenica, Europe's Worst Massacre Since World War II.* New York: Farrar, Straus and Giroux, 1997.

STOVER, ERIC, with photographs by GILLES PERESS. *The Graves: Srebrenica and Vukovar.* New York: Scalo, 1998.

SUDETIC, CHUCK. *Blood and Vengeance: One Family's Story of the War in Bosnia.* New York: Norton, 1998.

ARTICLES

BURNS, JOHN. "Aid Trucks Arrive in a Bosnian Town as Serbs Yield." *New York Times* (20 March 1993): 1.

_____. "Food Convoy Arrives in Bosnian Town." *New York Times* (29 March 1993): 8.

_____. "Standoff for Muslim Enclave in Bosnia." *New York Times* (23 April 1993): 12.

_____. "Serbs Reported Willing to Allow Muslims to Leave Overrun Area." *New York Times* (5 March 1993): 1.

_____. "Tense U.N. Forces Hold Fast as Serbs Demand They Quit Enclave." *New York Times* (27 April 1993): 6.

CARVER, TOM. "Srebrenica's Diaspora." *New Statesman* (16 July 1996): 22–23.

DANNER, MARK. "Bosnia: Breaking the Machine." *New York Review of Books* 45, no. 3 (19 February 1998): 41–45.

_____. "Bosnia: The Great Betrayal." *New York Review of Books* 45, no. 5 (26 March 1998): 40–52.

_____. "Clinton, the UN, and the Bosnian Disaster." *New York Review of Books* 44, no. 20 (18 December 1997): 65–81.

_____. "The Killing Fields of Bosnia." *New York Review of Books* 45, no. 14 (24 September 1998): 63–77.

_____. "The US and the Yugoslav Catastrophe." *New York Review of Books* 44, no. 18 (20 November 1997): 56–64.

ENGLEBERG, STEPHEN. "The Agony of Srebrenica." *New York Times* (29 November 1995).

JAGGER, BIANCA. "The Betrayal of Srebrenica." *The European* (25 September–1 October, 1997).

JUDAH, TIM. "Sarajevo Attacked as World Watches Srebrenica Siege." *London Times* (23 March 1993).

LANE, CHARLES. "The Fall of Srebrenica." *New Republic* 213, no. 7 (14 August 1995): 14–17.

_____. "The Memo." *New Republic* 213, no. 21 (20 November 1995): 16–18.

LEWIS, PAUL. "U.N. Visitors Say Srebrenica is 'an Open Jail.'" *New York Times* (26 April 1993): 8.

POMFRET, JOHN. "U.N. Delegation Visits Shell-Scarred Bosnian Enclave." *Washington Post* (26 April 1993): A13.

RIDING, ALAN. "France Finds a Hero in a Balkan Town." *New York Times* (20 March 1993): 4.

SUDETIC, CHUCK. "Serbs Overrun Muslim Enclave in Bosnia's East." *New York Times* (15 March 1993): 3.

_____. "Thousands Jam U.N. Trucks to Flee Bosnian Town." *New York Times* (30 March 1993): 6.

_____. "U.N. General Visits Besieged Bosnians." *New York Times* (7 March 1993): 10.

Traynor, Ian. " 'I Estimate That 20 to 30 People Are Dying of Starvation Every Day': British Doctor Witnesses Ethnic Cleansing in Besieged Bosnia." *The Guardian* (London) (15 March 1993): 1.

Vulliamy, Ed. "Dutch Ordered Bosnia Retreat." *The Observer* (9 February 1997): 5.

VIDEOS

"Safe Haven: The United Nations and the Betrayal of Srebrenica." (A Production of Tamouz Media. Producer/Director, Ilan Ziv). New York: First Run/Icarus Films, 1996. For more information, visit www.tamouz.com

REPORTS

The Betrayal of Srebrenica: Why Did the Massacre Happen? Will It Happen Again?
United States Congress. House Committee on International Relations. Subcommittee on International Operations and Human Rights. Washington: United States Government Printing Office, 1998.

To Bury My Brothers' Bones. London: Amnesty International, 1996. A Report on the Aftermath of the Fall of Srebrenica.

United Nations' Srebrenica Report [Report of the Secretary General Pursuant to General Assembly Resolution 53/35 (1998)]. New York: United Nations, 1999.

INTERNET SITES

Amnesty International
Balkans Coordination Group
www.amnesty-usa.org/group/balkans/

Community of Bosnia
www.students.haverford.edu/vfilipov/

Doctors without Borders/USA
www.dwb.org

Fellowship of Reconciliation
www.nonviolence.org/for/

Friends of Bosnia
www.crocker.com/~fob/

Human Rights Watch
www.hrw.org

Physicians for Human Rights
www.phrusa.org

Srebrenica Justice Campaign
ds.dial.pipex.com/srebrenica.justice/

Women of Srebrenica
www.srebrenica.org

All income from this publication will be used to assist Bosnian refugees from Srebrenica.
To support these efforts, please send your tax-deductible donation made payable to: Bosnian Resettlement Fund, 3310 S.Grand Blvd., St. Louis, Missouri, 63118.

after the fall ACKNOWLEDGMENTS

GRATEFUL APPRECIATION IS EXTENDED TO:

The Orić families for their openness, hospitality, and friendship;

Sam Landers for providing a dignified and beautiful layout;

Lejla Susic for her superb interpreting and translation;

David Rohde for his thoughtful contribution to this volume;

Ron Klutho and Alison Snape for their extraordinary efforts on behalf of the people of Srebrenica;

Ilan Ziv and Tamouz Media for their kind permission to use video imagery from "Safe Haven";

Kathryn Kissam for her enthusiastic endorsement of the project.

And to all those who supported and helped with this project, including: Davor and Josipa Šopf, Sead and Munevera Ramić, Mirsad and Fatma Salihović, Amir Jugović, Dijana and Chuck Groth, Eric Sandweiss, Myron Freedman, A.T. Stephens, John Wolford, Susan Beattie, Robin Machiran, Nancy McIlvaney, Margaret Koch, Safeta Ovčina, Hamdija and Rabia Jakubović, Eva Elvira Klonowski, Michael Sells, Sara Kahn, Bianca Jagger, Rabbi Robert Sternberg, Mira Tanna, Bill Ramsey, Fadil Mehmedović, Hamdija Ramić, Fr. Joseph Abramović, Muhamed Duraković, Katherine Bomberger, Mira Baratta, Gerry Wallman, Linda Valerian, Imam Muhamed Hasić, Batya Abramson-Goldstein, Nasja Meyer, Frances Benham, Sr. Paulette Weindel, Keith Doubt, Armin Karabegović, Adnan Jašarević, Amir Kundalić, Elvir Mandžukić, Edin Mandžukić, Adisa Selmanović, Tahir Čambiš, Željković family, Mehmedović family, Ibro Osmanović, Hedy Epstein, Leo and Jeanean Mitchell, Jean Parker and colleagues at Pius Library, Amra and Enes Kanlić, Katie Krcatovich, Harry O'Rourke, Semra Ramoševac, Rich Vaughn, Kelly Korenak, Suada Kovačević, Doug Hostetter, Noel Barrett, Raif and Hajrija Salihović, Farzad Wafapoor, Trish Curtis, Glenn Ruga, Husić family, Bećirović family, Sharon Pederson, Clayton Pape, Beth Morimoto, Aaron Lowin, Muratović family, Mary McCarthy, Virginia McCarthy, Almir Mutapčić, Lejla Mutapčić, Renate Hawkinberry, Lawrence Barmann, Ken Parker, Kym Hemley, Patti Hagen, Carole Knight, Lindsay Smith, Nancy Klepper, Katie Heit, Shelley Preston, Kemal Kurspahić, Jasminka and Dževad Hadžibegović, Art Sandler, Ann Haubrich, Jon Segal, Richard Byrne, John Mitchell and Ademir Korić.

Special thanks to Lee Sandweiss and the editorial staff of the Missouri Historical Society Press, especially Matt Heidenry and Cindy Alexander.

Finally, thanks to our families—Mary Mitchell, Kevin, Anne, and Kate McCarthy—and Gerry Weitz, for providing us the time to work on this project.

—Patrick McCarthy   Tom Maday

David Rohde was the first reporter to uncover direct evidence of atrocities following the fall of Srebrenica. While covering the Bosnian war for the *Christian Science Monitor*, Rohde visited the Srebrenica area several weeks after the massacres and located mass grave sites. In September 1995, he located and interviewed nine survivors of mass executions, including victims who placed General Ratko Mladić at three execution sites. In October, on a second visit, he found two additional mass graves but was arrested by Bosnian Serb police and imprisoned for ten days. Threatened with an espionage charge that carried a penalty from ten years in prison to death, Rohde was released only after U.S. Ambassador Richard Holbrooke and the Committee to Protect Journalists intervened on his behalf at the Balkan peace talks in Dayton, Ohio.

Rohde's coverage of the fall of Srebrenica has been credited with strengthening Western resolve in Bosnia and increasing pressure to apprehend Bosnian Serb leaders indicted by the International Criminal Tribunal in the Hague. Awarded the 1996 Pulitzer Prize for international reporting, Rohde is author of *Endgame: the Betrayal and Fall of Srebrenica* (1997). He is currently a reporter for the *New York Times*.

Interpreter and translator **Lejla Susic** is from the city of Mostar in Bosnia-Herzegovina. After fleeing as a refugee in 1993, Susic completed her undergraduate studies in political science at Iona College of New York, with scholarship assistance from the Bosnian Student Project. Susic was a member of the executive board of the Association of Students from Bosnia-Herzegovina and a spokesperson for Bosnian students to the World University Service.

Susic moved to St. Louis in 1995 to be reunited with her parents, who came to the United States as refugees. In St. Louis, Susic obtained her master's degree in International Relations at Webster University. Susic is now Language Team Leader for Language Access Metro Project (LAMP), a Catholic Social Services–sponsored program which provides interpreting, translation, and cross cultural services for Bosnian and other refugees.